Multiplying and Dividing Fractions

Grades 5–8

Authors: Schyrlet Cameron and Carolyn Craig
Editors: Mary Dieterich and Sarah M. Anderson
Proofreader: Margaret Brown

COPYRIGHT © 2013 Mark Twain Media, Inc.

ISBN 978-1-62223-007-5

Printing No. CD-404184

Mark Twain Media, Inc., Publishers
Distributed by Carson-Dellosa Publishing LLC

Table of Contents

Introduction to the Teacher

Fractions are an integral part of performing higher math skills. What is learned at one grade level is built upon at the next grade level. The Common Core State Standards for Mathematics suggests part of the instructional time for grades five through seven should focus on fractions. In the eighth grade, students should be able to apply previous understanding of fractions to solve problems involving mathematical expressions and equations and statistics and probability.

Multiplying and Dividing Fractions targets the basic concepts needed to build a solid foundation for understanding and performing fractional skills involving higher math. The structure of the content and presentation of concepts and skills in this book supports the Common Core State Standards for Mathematics.

This book is divided into five units. The units cover fractional concepts and the basic operations of multiplying and dividing fractions and mixed numbers. Using fractions with percents, probability, and ratios is also covered. Units are divided into several lessons. Each lesson covers one concept. The format of this book is designed to facilitate lesson planning.

- **Lesson Introduction** is designed as a teacher-guided introduction of the lesson's concepts and skills. Each page includes the lesson objective, vocabulary and definitions, overview of skills and concepts to be taught, example problems with clear and concise explanations, sample problems to try with the students, and a real-world connection for the skill.

- **Practice** is a set of exercises involving concepts and skills presented in the Lesson Introduction.

- **Assessment** is an evaluation of what the student has learned in each Unit. Each assessment is presented in standardized-test format.

- **Learning Stations Activity** is a set of activities that allow students to apply the concepts they have learned about fractions.

- **Glossary of Terms** is an organized list of the vocabulary presented in the book.

- **Daily Math Review** are sets of problems that can be used to review concepts and skills involving fractions.

Multiplying and Dividing Fractions offers teachers a wide variety of instructional options to meet the diverse learning styles of middle-school students. The book can be used to introduce, review, or reinforce fractional skills and concepts needed by students in grades 5–8. The lessons can be used for whole-group or small-group instruction, independent practice, or homework. It can be used to supplement or enhance the regular classroom curriculum or with Title I instruction.

Downloadable versions of the Lesson Introduction pages can be found at www.carsondellosa. com. Search for product number CD-404184. On the *Multiplying and Dividing Fractions* product page, click on the Resources tab. Click on the file and download the pages for free. These can be easily used with a classroom whiteboard, projection device, or computer.

Common Core State Standards Matrix

Standards for Mathematical Practice

Units of Study	Standards for Grades 5–8							
	Make sense of problems and persevere in solving them.	Reason abstractly and quantitatively.	Construct viable arguments and critique the reasoning of others.	Model with mathematics.	Use appropriate tools strategically.	Attend to precision.	Look for and make use of structure.	Look for and express regularity in repeated reasoning.
Fraction Basics	X	X		X	X	X	X	
Multiplying Fractions and Mixed Numbers	X	X		X	X	X	X	
Dividing Fractions and Mixed Numbers	X	X		X	X	X	X	
Fractions and Decimals	X	X		X	X	X	X	
Percent/Probability/Ratios	X	X		X	X	X	X	

Standards for Mathematical Content

Units of Study	Standards for Grades 5–8																			
	5.OA	5.NBT	5.NF	5.MD	5.G	6.RP	6.NS	6.EE	6.G	6.SP	7.RP	7.NS	7.EE	7.G	7.SP	8.NS	8.EE	8.F	8.G	8.SP
Fraction Basics			X	X			X					X				X				
Multiplying Fractions and Mixed Numbers			X	X			X					X				X				
Dividing Fractions and Mixed Numbers			X	X			X					X				X				
Fractions and Decimals		X				X				X	X									
Percent/Probability/Ratios						X				X	X				X					

Lesson Introduction: The Meaning of Fractions

Common Core State Standard	Objective
• Fifth Grade: 5.NF.3-7 • Sixth Grade: 6.NS.1, 6.NS.4 • Seventh Grade: 7.NS.1 • Eighth Grade: 8.NS.1	• Read and write proper fractions, mixed numbers, and improper fractions in standard and word form.

Vocabulary
denominator, fraction, fraction bar, improper fractions, mixed number, numerator, proper fraction, standard form, whole number, word form

Overview
There are three types of fractions: proper fractions, improper fractions, and mixed numbers.

A **proper fraction** expresses a whole divided into any number of equal parts. It is a number usually expressed in the form a/b. The bottom number of a fraction is the **denominator**. It tells you how many equal parts the whole is divided into. The top number of the fraction is the **numerator**. It tells how many equal parts of the whole you have. The numerator is less than the denominator in a proper fraction. A **fraction bar** is a line separating the numerator and denominator of a fraction and stands for division.

An **improper fraction** is a fraction in which the numerator is greater than or equal to the denominator.

A **mixed number** is a whole number and a fraction. A **whole number** is a counting number.

A fraction can be written in **standard form** or **word form**. A fraction written in standard form is written as a number. A fraction written in word form is written as words.

Three types of Fractions

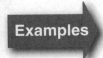

Proper Fraction	Improper Fraction	Mixed Number
$\dfrac{3}{4}$	$\dfrac{7}{3}$ or $\dfrac{2}{2}$	$2\dfrac{4}{5}$

Problems to Try

a. Write the standard form of four-sixths.

Answer: $\dfrac{4}{6}$

b. Write the word form of $\dfrac{11}{9}$.

Answer: eleven-ninths

c. Write a mixed number for the picture.

Answer: $1\dfrac{3}{4}$

Real-World Connection
A pizza cook has to be able to read and understand fractions. Example: A customer's order might read "large pizza, 1/2 pepperoni, 2/5 mushrooms and 1/10 bacon."

Name: _____ Date: _____

Practice: The Meaning of Fractions

1. Write a fraction for the picture.

_____

2. Write a mixed number for the picture.

_____

3. Write an improper fraction for the picture.

_____

4. Write the word form of $4\frac{2}{3}$. _____

5. Write the word form of $\frac{5}{6}$. _____

6. Write the word form of $\frac{6}{4}$. _____

7. Write the word form of $1\frac{3}{10}$. _____

8. Write the word form of $\frac{2}{2}$. _____

9. Write the standard form of ten and one-sixth. _____

10. Write the standard form of one-fourth. _____

11. Write the standard form of twelve and two-thirds. _____

12. Write the standard form of nine-ninths. _____

13. Write the standard form of three-fourths. _____

14. Write the standard form of five-thirds. _____

15. Write the standard form of six-fifths. _____

Lesson Introduction: Simplifying Fractions

Common Core State Standard	Objective
• Fifth Grade: 5.NF.3-7 • Sixth Grade: 6.NS.1, 6.NS.4 • Seventh Grade: 7.NS.1 • Eighth Grade: 8.NS.1	• Write fractions in lowest terms. • Find the factors of numbers. • Find the greatest common factor of two numbers.

Vocabulary

common factor, equivalent, factors, greatest common factor, simplest form, simplify

Overview

Every number has factors. The **factors** of a number divide that number evenly. The factors of 18 are 1, 2, 3, 6, 9, and 18.

A number that is a factor of two or more numbers is a **common factor** of those numbers. The largest common factor of two or more numbers is called the **greatest common factor (GCF)**.

A fraction is in its **simplest form** if 1 is the only number that will divide both the numerator and the denominator. If a fraction is not in simplest form, you can reduce it. **Simplify** means to reduce a fraction to the lowest **equivalent**, or equal fraction. To simplify a fraction, divide both the numerator and the denominator by the greatest common factor. Then, rewrite the fraction.

Finding Greatest Common Factor (GCF)

> What is the greatest common factor of 8 and 12?
>   factors of 8: 1, 2, **4**, and 8
>   factors of 12: 1, 2, 3, **4**, 6, and 12
>   The greatest common factor of 8 and 12 is 4.

Simplifying Fractions

Divide both the numerator and the denominator by the greatest common factor.

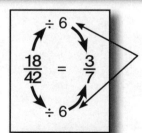

Greatest common factor of 18 and 42 is 6.

Problems to Try

a.   What is the greatest common factor of 36 and 48? **Answer:** 12

b.   Simplify $\frac{3}{15}$. **Answer:** $\frac{1}{5}$

Real-World Connection

You use fractions every time you look at a clock. The expression "half past the hour" includes a fraction $\left(\frac{1}{2}\right)$.

Name: _____   Date: _____

Practice: Simplifying Fractions

1. List the factors of 24. _____

2. List the factors of 8. _____

3. List the factors of 18. _____

4. List the factors of 48. _____

5. List the factors of 75. _____

6. What is the greatest common factor of 14 and 28? _____

7. What is the greatest common factor of 18 and 30? _____

8. What is the greatest common factor of 24 and 40? _____

For problems 9–16, simplify the fraction.

9. $\frac{6}{8}$ = _____

10. $\frac{9}{15}$ = _____

11. $\frac{15}{35}$ = _____

12. $\frac{12}{18}$ = _____

13. $\frac{8}{12}$ = _____

14. $\frac{12}{24}$ = _____

15. $\frac{14}{35}$ = _____

16. $\frac{14}{36}$ = _____

Lesson Introduction: Converting Mixed Numbers and Improper Fractions

Common Core State Standard	Objective
• Fifth Grade: 5.NF.3-7 • Sixth Grade: 6.NS.1, 6.NS.4 • Seventh Grade: 7.NS.1 • Eighth Grade: 8.NS.1	• Convert mixed numbers to improper fractions. • Convert improper fractions to mixed numbers.

Vocabulary

convert, denominator, improper fraction, mixed numbers, numerator, whole number

Overview

A **mixed number** is a whole number and a fraction. A **whole number** is a counting number. An **improper fraction** is a fraction in which the numerator is greater than the denominator. The **numerator** of a fraction is the top number, and the **denominator** is the bottom number. It is easy to **convert** or change a mixed number to an improper fraction or to change improper fractions to mixed numbers.

Converting Mixed Numbers to Improper Fractions

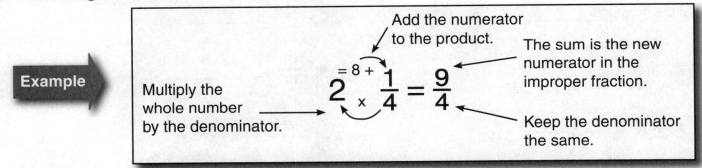

Converting Improper Fractions to Mixed Numbers

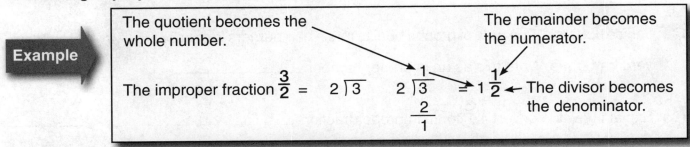

Problems to Try

a. Write an improper fraction for $2\frac{5}{7}$.   **Answer:** $\frac{19}{7}$

b. Write a mixed number for $\frac{18}{5}$.   **Answer:** $3\frac{3}{5}$

Real-World Connection

Aerospace engineers use fractions when drawing the blueprints used to build aircraft.

Name: _____ Date: _____

Practice: Converting Mixed Numbers and Improper Fractions

Directions: Convert the mixed numbers to improper fractions. Simplify the answers.

Directions: Convert the improper fractions to mixed or whole numbers. Simplify the answers.

1. $7\frac{4}{5}$ = _____

2. $1\frac{8}{9}$ = _____

3. $10\frac{4}{5}$ = _____

4. $1\frac{7}{10}$ = _____

5. $6\frac{2}{3}$ = _____

6. $3\frac{5}{70}$ = _____

7. $9\frac{5}{6}$ = _____

8. $4\frac{3}{8}$ = _____

9. $\frac{10}{3}$ = _____

10. $\frac{4}{2}$ = _____

11. $\frac{3}{3}$ = _____

12. $\frac{43}{7}$ = _____

13. $\frac{29}{4}$ = _____

14. $\frac{23}{3}$ = _____

15. $\frac{13}{13}$ = _____

16. $\frac{19}{10}$ = _____

Apply

17. Janice bought $4\frac{3}{4}$ pounds of ground beef to make hamburgers for a back-yard barbeque. Write this as an improper number. _____

18. Explain how to convert $4\frac{3}{4}$ to an improper fraction. _____

_____

_____

_____

Name: _____   Date: _____

Unit Assessment: Fraction Basics

Directions: Fill in the bubble next to the correct answer for each multiple choice question.

1. What fraction of the circle is shaded?

  ○ **a.** $\frac{1}{6}$

  ○ **b.** $\frac{5}{6}$

  ○ **c.** $\frac{4}{6}$

  ○ **d.** $\frac{2}{6}$

2. What is the improper fraction for the model?

  ○ **a.** $\frac{17}{5}$

  ○ **b.** $\frac{17}{6}$

  ○ **c.** $2\frac{9}{16}$

  ○ **d.** $2\frac{5}{6}$

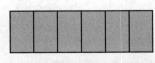

3. What is the mixed number for the model?

  ○ **a.** $1\frac{1}{3}$

  ○ **b.** $2\frac{1}{4}$

  ○ **c.** $2\frac{1}{3}$

  ○ **d.** $2\frac{2}{3}$

4. What is the word form of $5\frac{4}{6}$?

  ○ **a.** four-fifths

  ○ **b.** five and six-fourths

  ○ **c.** four-sixths and five

  ○ **d.** five and four-sixths

5. What is the standard form of thirteen and three-fourths?

  ○ **a.** $13\frac{1}{2}$

  ○ **b.** $13\frac{2}{4}$

  ○ **c.** $13\frac{3}{4}$

  ○ **d.** $14\frac{1}{4}$

6. Which is the complete list of factors for 12?

  ○ **a.** 0, 1, 2, 3, 4, 6, and 12

  ○ **b.** 1, 2, 3, 4, 6, and 12

  ○ **c.** 2, 3, 4, 6, and 12

  ○ **d.** 0, 1, 2, 3, 4, and 6

Name: _____ Date: _____

Unit Assessment: Fraction Basics (cont.)

7. What is the greatest common factor for 14 and 21?

   ○ **a.** 2

   ○ **b.** 3

   ○ **c.** 7

   ○ **d.** 14

8. Simplify $\frac{6}{12}$.

   ○ **a.** $\frac{1}{4}$

   ○ **b.** $\frac{1}{3}$

   ○ **c.** $\frac{1}{2}$

   ○ **d.** 1

9. Simplify $6\frac{12}{18}$.

   ○ **a.** $6\frac{2}{3}$

   ○ **b.** $6\frac{3}{4}$

   ○ **c.** $6\frac{1}{4}$

   ○ **d.** $7\frac{1}{3}$

10. Convert $5\frac{2}{3}$ to an improper fraction.

   ○ **a.** $\frac{2}{3}$

   ○ **b.** $\frac{10}{3}$

   ○ **c.** $\frac{13}{3}$

   ○ **d.** $\frac{17}{3}$

11. How is $\frac{14}{6}$ written as a mixed number?

   ○ **a.** $2\frac{3}{4}$

   ○ **b.** $2\frac{1}{2}$

   ○ **c.** $2\frac{1}{4}$

   ○ **d.** $2\frac{1}{3}$

12. Simplify $\frac{6}{6}$.

   ○ **a.** $\frac{1}{2}$

   ○ **b.** 1

   ○ **c.** $1\frac{1}{2}$

   ○ **d.** 2

Lesson Introduction: Multiplying a Fraction by a Fraction

Common Core State Standard	Objective
• Fifth Grade: 5.NF.3, 5.NF.4, 5.NF.6 • Sixth Grade: 6.NS.1 • Seventh Grade: 7.NS.2, 7.NS.3 • Eighth Grade: 8.NS.1	• Multiply a fraction by a fraction. • Simplify the product of two fractions to lowest terms.

Vocabulary

denominators, fraction, numerators, simplify

Overview

A **fraction** expresses a whole divided into any number of equal parts. It is a number usually expressed in the form a/b. To multiply fractions, first multiply the **numerators**, or the top numbers. Then multiply the **denominators**, or the bottom numbers. If possible, simplify the answer. **Simplify** means to rewrite the answer in its lowest terms.

Multiplying a Fraction by a Fraction

Example

Multiply the numerators.

$$\frac{3}{4} \times \frac{2}{3} = \frac{3 \times 2}{4 \times 3} = \frac{6}{12} = \frac{1}{2}$$

If possible, simplify the answer.

Multiply the denominators.

Problems to Try

a. $\frac{1}{3} \times \frac{1}{2} =$

Answer: $\frac{1}{6}$

b. $\frac{2}{4} \times \frac{2}{3} \times \frac{1}{2} =$

Answer: $\frac{4}{24} = \frac{1}{6}$

Real-World Connection

The gas gauge in a car is based on fractions. If the gas tank on a car holds 20 gallons of gas, and the gauge indicates $\frac{1}{4}$ tank, you have 5 gallons of gas.

Name: _____ Date: _____

Practice: Multiplying a Fraction by a Fraction

Directions: Solve the problems below by multiplying the fractions. Simplify the answers.

1. $\frac{7}{8} \times \frac{5}{6} =$ _____

2. $\frac{4}{5} \times \frac{1}{2} =$ _____

3. $\frac{3}{8} \times \frac{3}{4} =$ _____

4. $\frac{3}{5} \times \frac{3}{10} =$ _____

5. $\frac{3}{5} \times \frac{7}{8} =$ _____

6. $\frac{7}{8} \times \frac{4}{5} =$ _____

7. $\frac{5}{8} \times \frac{3}{4} =$ _____

8. $\frac{4}{5} \times \frac{2}{5} =$ _____

9. $\frac{5}{6} \times \frac{1}{12} =$ _____

10. $\frac{3}{5} \times \frac{2}{3} =$ _____

11. $\frac{2}{5} \times \frac{7}{10} =$ _____

12. $\frac{4}{5} \times \frac{5}{6} =$ _____

13. $\frac{5}{6} \times \frac{3}{10} =$ _____

14. $\frac{3}{5} \times \frac{7}{10} =$ _____

15. $\frac{3}{8} \times \frac{1}{2} =$ _____

16. $\frac{4}{5} \times \frac{2}{3} =$ _____

Apply

17. Kathy's cookie recipe calls for $\frac{2}{3}$ cup of sugar. How much sugar would she use to make $\frac{2}{3}$ of a batch of cookies? _____

18. Explain how you got the answer for problem 17. _____

_____

_____

_____

Lesson Introduction: Multiplying Fractions and Whole Numbers

Common Core State Standard	Objective
• Fifth Grade: 5.NF.3, 5.NF.4, 5.NF.6 • Sixth Grade: 6.NS.1 • Seventh Grade: 7.NS.2, 7.NS.3 • Eighth Grade: 8.NS.1	• Multiply a fraction with a whole number. • Simplify the product of two fractions to lowest terms.

Vocabulary

denominator, fraction, numerators, simplify, whole number

Overview

A **fraction** expresses a whole divided into any number of equal parts. It is a number usually expressed in the form a/b. A **whole number** is a counting number, such as 1, 2, or 3.

To multiply fractions and whole numbers, first rewrite the whole number as a fraction by placing the whole number over the number 1. Next, multiply the **numerators**, or the top numbers. Then multiply the **denominators**, or the bottom numbers. If possible, simplify the answer. **Simplify** means to rewrite the answer in its lowest terms.

Multiplying Fractions and Whole Numbers

Example

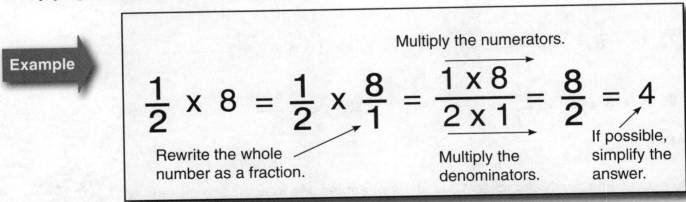

Problems to Try

a. $\frac{1}{4} \times 12 =$

Answer: 3

b. $7 \times \frac{2}{5} =$

Answer: $2\frac{4}{5}$

Real-World Connection

Several fast-food restaurants sell quarter-pound hamburgers. If you understand fractions, you can figure out how many ounces of beef you will get in your hamburger.

Name: _____ Date: _____

Practice: Multiplying Fractions and Whole Numbers

Directions: Solve the problems below by multiplying the fractions. Simplify the answers.

1. $\frac{1}{8} \times 8 =$ _____

2. $\frac{1}{2} \times 23 =$ _____

3. $5 \times \frac{1}{10} =$ _____

4. $16 \times \frac{2}{3} =$ _____

5. $\frac{1}{3} \times 17 =$ _____

6. $6 \times \frac{3}{4} =$ _____

7. $12 \times \frac{7}{8} =$ _____

8. $\frac{1}{6} \times 3 =$ _____

9. $19 \times \frac{3}{5} =$ _____

10. $11 \times \frac{5}{6} =$ _____

11. $\frac{1}{4} \times 31 =$ _____

12. $\frac{1}{8} \times 12 =$ _____

13. $25 \times \frac{1}{5} =$ _____

14. $\frac{7}{8} \times 14 =$ _____

15. $\frac{3}{10} \times 21 =$ _____

16. $35 \times \frac{4}{5} =$ _____

Apply

17. On Saturday, Nick picked 10 bushels of apples. Monday, Shane picked $\frac{1}{3}$ as many apples as Nick. How many bushels of apples did Shane pick on Monday? _____

18. Explain how you got the answer for problem 17. _____

_____

_____

_____

Lesson Introduction: Multiplying Mixed Numbers

Common Core State Standard	Objective
• Fifth Grade: 5.NF.3, 5.NF.4, 5.NF.6 • Sixth Grade: 6.NS.1 • Seventh Grade: 7.NS.2, 7.NS.3 • Eighth Grade: 8.NS.1	• Multiply mixed numbers. • Convert mixed numbers to improper fractions. • Convert improper fractions to mixed numbers. • Simplify products to lowest terms.

Vocabulary

convert, denominators, fraction, improper fraction, mixed number, numerators, simplify, whole number

Overview

A **fraction** expresses a whole divided into any number of equal parts. It is a number usually expressed in the form *a/b*. A **whole number** is a counting number, such as 1, 2, or 3. A **mixed number** is a whole number and a fraction. A mixed number can be converted to an improper fraction. An **improper fraction** is a fraction in which the numerator is greater than the denominator. To **convert** means to change.

An improper fraction can be converted to a mixed number by dividing the numerator by the denominator. To convert a mixed number to an improper fraction, first multiply the whole number by the **denominator** or bottom number of the fraction. Add the **numerator** or top number to the product. The sum is the new numerator in your improper fraction. Keep the denominator the same.

To multiply mixed numbers, first convert the mixed numbers to improper fractions. If one of the numbers being multiplied is a whole number, rewrite the whole number as a fraction by placing the whole number over the number 1. Next, multiply the numerators. Then multiply the denominators. If possible, simplify the answer. **Simplify** means to rewrite the answer in its lowest terms.

Multiplying Mixed Numbers

Example →

$$3\frac{1}{2} \times 2\frac{1}{2}$$

Convert the mixed numbers to improper fractions and multiply.

$$\frac{7}{2} \times \frac{5}{2} = \frac{7 \times 5}{2 \times 2} = \frac{35}{4} = 8\frac{3}{6} = 8\frac{1}{2}$$

Problems to Try

a. $4\frac{1}{5} \times 2 =$ **Answer:** $8\frac{2}{5}$

b. $8\frac{2}{3} \times 1\frac{1}{2} =$ **Answer:** 13

Real-World Connection

When you take your car to an automotive shop, the mechanics might use a $\frac{9}{16}$-inch wrench or $1\frac{7}{8}$-inch socket to repair your car.

Name: _____ Date: _____

Practice: Multiplying Mixed Numbers

Directions: Solve the problems below by multiplying the fractions. Simplify the answers.

1. $5\frac{5}{6} \times 2\frac{1}{7} =$ _____

2. $4\frac{4}{5} \times 3\frac{1}{8} =$ _____

3. $1\frac{2}{3} \times 2\frac{1}{3} =$ _____

4. $1\frac{3}{5} \times 2\frac{1}{4} =$ _____

5. $2\frac{1}{2} \times 2\frac{2}{5} =$ _____

6. $3\frac{1}{2} \times 2\frac{1}{4} =$ _____

7. $1\frac{2}{3} \times 2\frac{1}{6} =$ _____

8. $2\frac{1}{10} \times 4\frac{2}{7} =$ _____

9. $3\frac{1}{5} \times 6\frac{1}{4} =$ _____

10. $1\frac{4}{5} \times 6\frac{7}{8} =$ _____

11. $3\frac{1}{2} \times 3\frac{1}{2} =$ _____

12. $2\frac{1}{7} \times 5\frac{1}{4} =$ _____

13. $5\frac{5}{9} \times 2\frac{1}{4} =$ _____

14. $5\frac{1}{3} \times 3\frac{1}{8} =$ _____

15. $3\frac{1}{2} \times 1\frac{1}{7} =$ _____

16. $1\frac{1}{8} \times 3\frac{2}{3} =$ _____

Apply

17. Last week, Joslyn walked $3\frac{1}{2}$ miles. This week, she plans on walking $1\frac{1}{5}$ times as far as last week. How many miles does Joslyn plan on walking this week? _____

18. Explain how you got the answer for problem 17. _____

_____

_____

_____

Lesson Introduction: Multiplying Fractions and Mixed Numbers: A Shortcut

Common Core State Standard	Objective
• Fifth Grade: 5.NF.3, 5.NF.4, 5.NF.6 • Sixth Grade: 6.NS.1 • Seventh Grade: 7.NS.2, 7.NS.3 • Eighth Grade: 8.NS.1	• Cross-cancel to make multiplying fractions easier to work with.

Vocabulary

cross-cancel, fraction

Overview

A **fraction** expresses a whole divided into any number of equal parts. It is a number usually expressed in the form a/b. When working with fractions, you can cross-cancel to make the problem easier to work with. Instead of simplifying the fraction at the end of the problem, you can cross-cancel before you multiply. **Cross-cancel** means to simplify before you multiply.

Cross-Cancel

Examples

$$\frac{2}{3} \times \frac{1}{2} = \frac{\cancel{2}^{1} \times 1}{3 \times \cancel{2}_{1}} = \frac{1}{3}$$

Simplify by removing the common factors before multiplying.

$$3\frac{1}{8} \times 4\frac{4}{5} = \frac{25}{8} \times \frac{24}{5} = \frac{\cancel{25}^{5}}{\cancel{8}_{1}} \times \frac{\cancel{24}^{3}}{\cancel{5}_{1}} = \frac{15}{1} = 15$$

Problems to Try

a. $\frac{2}{3} \times \frac{7}{10} =$ **Answer:** $\frac{7}{15}$

b. $1\frac{5}{6} \times \frac{5}{11} \times 2\frac{1}{4} =$ **Answer:** $1\frac{7}{8}$

Real-World Connection

Recipes often call for $\frac{1}{2}$, $\frac{1}{4}$, and $\frac{1}{3}$-cup measurements of ingredients. If you decide to double or triple your favorite chocolate chip cookie recipe, you will need to have an understanding of how to multiply fractions.

Name: _____   Date: _____

Practice: Multiplying Fractions and Mixed Numbers: A Shortcut

Directions: Solve the problems below by multiplying the fractions. Use cross-canceling where possible. Simplify the answers.

1. $\frac{4}{5} \times \frac{3}{8} =$ _____

2. $\frac{4}{9} \times \frac{1}{2} =$ _____

3. $3\frac{1}{2} \times \frac{6}{7} =$ _____

4. $\frac{7}{9} \times \frac{3}{5} =$ _____

5. $3\frac{1}{5} \times \frac{1}{4} =$ _____

6. $\frac{6}{7} \times \frac{7}{8} =$ _____

7. $1\frac{5}{9} \times \frac{3}{5} =$ _____

8. $\frac{3}{8} \times \frac{6}{7} =$ _____

9. $\frac{2}{5} \times 2\frac{3}{4} =$ _____

10. $1\frac{4}{5} \times \frac{5}{6} =$ _____

11. $\frac{5}{8} \times \frac{3}{10} =$ _____

12. $6\frac{1}{4} \times \frac{2}{5} =$ _____

13. $\frac{5}{16} \times \frac{8}{9} =$ _____

14. $\frac{4}{5} \times \frac{7}{12} =$ _____

15. $\frac{3}{16} \times 5\frac{1}{3} =$ _____

16. $2\frac{5}{6} \times \frac{8}{9} =$ _____

Apply

17. On Tuesday, Mona's Cookie Shack sold $\frac{2}{3}$ as many chocolate chip cookies as sugar cookies. If they sold 3 trays of sugar cookies, how many trays of chocolate chip cookies did they sell? _____

18. Explain how you got the answer for problem 17. _____

_____

_____

_____

Name: _____ Date: _____

Unit Assessment: Multiplying Fractions and Mixed Numbers

Directions: Fill in the bubble next to the correct answer for each multiple choice question.

1. $\frac{3}{8} \times \frac{7}{10} =$

- ○ a. $\frac{1}{4}$
- ○ b. $\frac{21}{80}$
- ○ c. $\frac{9}{32}$
- ○ d. $\frac{21}{40}$

4. $5 \times 3\frac{1}{6} =$

- ○ a. $25\frac{5}{6}$
- ○ b. $15\frac{5}{6}$
- ○ c. $16\frac{1}{4}$
- ○ d. $16\frac{3}{4}$

2. $\frac{3}{4} \times \frac{6}{8} =$

- ○ a. $\frac{9}{16}$
- ○ b. $\frac{3}{4}$
- ○ c. $\frac{3}{16}$
- ○ d. $\frac{9}{32}$

5. $4\frac{2}{3} \times \frac{1}{7} =$

- ○ a. $5\frac{1}{2}$
- ○ b. $\frac{3}{4}$
- ○ c. $\frac{2}{3}$
- ○ d. $\frac{1}{7}$

3. $3 \times 2\frac{5}{6} =$

- ○ a. $5\frac{2}{3}$
- ○ b. $6\frac{1}{2}$
- ○ c. $8\frac{1}{2}$
- ○ d. $7\frac{5}{6}$

6. $\frac{9}{14} \times \frac{7}{9} =$

- ○ a. $\frac{2}{3}$
- ○ b. $\frac{3}{5}$
- ○ c. $1\frac{5}{7}$
- ○ d. $\frac{1}{2}$

Unit Assessment: Multiplying Fractions and Mixed Numbers (cont.)

7. $1\frac{1}{7} \times 3\frac{1}{2} =$

  ○ **a.** 5

  ○ **b.** 4

  ○ **c.** 56

  ○ **d.** $7\frac{1}{4}$

8. $6 \times 1\frac{3}{4} =$

  ○ **a.** $10\frac{1}{2}$

  ○ **b.** $1\frac{1}{2}$

  ○ **c.** $11\frac{1}{2}$

  ○ **d.** $7\frac{2}{3}$

9. $5\frac{1}{2} \times \frac{1}{3} =$

  ○ **a.** $1\frac{2}{3}$

  ○ **b.** $2\frac{5}{6}$

  ○ **c.** $2\frac{1}{2}$

  ○ **d.** $1\frac{5}{6}$

10. $\frac{9}{10} \times \frac{5}{12} =$

  ○ **a.** $\frac{7}{8}$

  ○ **b.** $\frac{3}{8}$

  ○ **c.** $\frac{5}{8}$

  ○ **d.** $\frac{3}{4}$

11. $\frac{5}{6} \times \frac{9}{10} \times \frac{2}{3} =$

  ○ **a.** $\frac{2}{3}$

  ○ **b.** $\frac{3}{4}$

  ○ **c.** $\frac{1}{2}$

  ○ **d.** $\frac{8}{9}$

12. $\frac{8}{9} \times \frac{3}{4} \times \frac{6}{7} =$

  ○ **a.** $\frac{5}{9}$

  ○ **b.** $\frac{7}{20}$

  ○ **c.** $\frac{4}{7}$

  ○ **d.** $\frac{5}{7}$

Lesson Introduction: Reciprocals

Common Core State Standard	Objective
• Fifth Grade: 5.NF.3, 5.NF.7 • Sixth Grade: 6.NS.1 • Seventh Grade: 7.NS.2, 7.NS.3 • Eighth Grade: 8.NS.1	• Find the reciprocal of whole numbers, fractions, and mixed numbers.

Vocabulary

fraction, denominator, numerator, improper fraction, mixed number, reciprocal, whole number

Overview

One number is the **reciprocal** of another if their product is 1. A **whole number** is a counting number, such as 1, 2, or 3. A **fraction** expresses a whole divided into any number of equal parts. It is a number usually expressed in the form a/b. An **improper fraction** is a fraction in which the **numerator** (the top number) is greater than or equal to the **denominator** (the bottom number). A **mixed number** is a whole number and a fraction.

Finding the Reciprocal

Examples →

The reciprocal of a whole number is obtained by placing the whole number over the number 1, making a fraction. Next, invert the fraction or flip the numerator and the denominator.

The reciprocal of 4 is $\frac{1}{4}$, since $\frac{4}{1} \times \frac{1}{4} = 1$.

The reciprocal of a fraction is obtained by inverting the fraction or by flipping the numerator and the denominator.

The reciprocal of $\frac{3}{4}$ is $\frac{4}{3}$, since $\frac{3}{4} \times \frac{4}{3} = 1$.

The reciprocal of a mixed number is obtained by converting the mixed number to an improper fraction and then inverting the improper fraction.

The reciprocal of $1\frac{1}{2}$ is $\frac{2}{3}$, since $1\frac{1}{2} = \frac{3}{2}$ and $\frac{3}{2} \times \frac{2}{3} = 1$.

Problems to Try

a. Find the reciprocal of 10. **Answer:** $\frac{1}{10}$

b. Find the reciprocal of $\frac{1}{5}$. **Answer:** $\frac{5}{1}$

c. Find the reciprocal of $2\frac{4}{5}$. **Answer:** $\frac{5}{14}$

Real-World Connection

Musical notes tell a musician which notes to play, when to play them, and how to play them. Examples of musical notes are $\frac{1}{1}$ (whole), $\frac{1}{2}$ (half), $\frac{1}{4}$ (quarter), $\frac{1}{8}$ (eighth), $\frac{1}{16}$ (sixteenth), and the very rare $\frac{1}{32}$ (thirty-second).

Name: _____ Date: _____

Practice: Reciprocals

Directions: Write the reciprocal for the fractions, whole numbers, and mixed numbers.

1. $\frac{3}{7}$ _____

2. $\frac{7}{8}$ _____

3. 7 _____

4. $\frac{5}{6}$ _____

5. $\frac{4}{5}$ _____

6. $\frac{2}{3}$ _____

7. 5 _____

8. $\frac{1}{12}$ _____

9. $1\frac{1}{4}$ _____

10. $9\frac{3}{4}$ _____

11. 21 _____

12. $14\frac{1}{2}$ _____

13. $9\frac{3}{5}$ _____

14. 73 _____

15. $5\frac{1}{6}$ _____

16. $10\frac{1}{3}$ _____

Apply

17. The reciprocal of $2\frac{3}{4}$ is $\frac{4}{11}$. Explain. _____

_____

_____

_____

Lesson Introduction: Dividing by Fractions

Common Core State Standard	Objective
• Fifth Grade: 5.NF.3, 5.NF.7 • Sixth Grade: 6.NS.1 • Seventh Grade: 7.NS.2, 7.NS.3 • Eighth Grade: 8.NS.1	• Find the reciprocal of a fraction. • Divide a fraction by a fraction. • Simplify answer to lowest terms.

Vocabulary
denominator, fraction, inverting, numerators, reciprocal, simplify, whole number

Overview
A **fraction** expresses a whole divided into any number of equal parts. It is a number usually expressed in the form *a/b*. One number is the **reciprocal** of another if their product is 1. The reciprocal of a fraction is obtained by **inverting** the fraction or by flipping the **numerator** (top number) and the **denominator** (bottom number). **Simplify** means to rewrite the answer in its lowest terms.

When dividing a fraction by a fraction, first invert the second fraction. This fraction is now a reciprocal. Change the division sign to a multiplication sign. Multiply the two fractions. If possible, simplify the answer.

Dividing Fractions

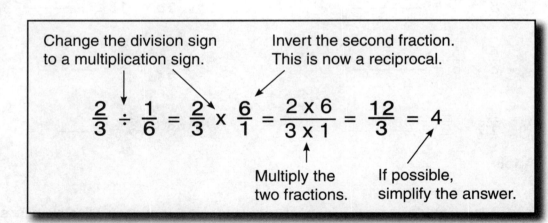

Example

Change the division sign to a multiplication sign.

Invert the second fraction. This is now a reciprocal.

$$\frac{2}{3} \div \frac{1}{6} = \frac{2}{3} \times \frac{6}{1} = \frac{2 \times 6}{3 \times 1} = \frac{12}{3} = 4$$

Multiply the two fractions.

If possible, simplify the answer.

Problems to Try

a. $\frac{1}{4} \div \frac{1}{3} =$ **Answer:** $\frac{3}{4}$

b. $\frac{1}{2} \div \frac{2}{5} =$ **Answer:** $1\frac{1}{4}$

Real-World Connection
Veneer is a wood product made of thin layers of wood glued together. It is commonly used in furniture manufacturing. Woodworkers measure the thickness of veneers in fractions such as $\frac{3}{32}$ or $\frac{1}{40}$ of an inch.

Name: _____   Date: _____

Practice: Dividing by Fractions

Directions: Solve the problems below by dividing the fractions. Simplify the answers.

1. $\dfrac{8}{9} \div \dfrac{1}{3} =$ _____

2. $\dfrac{6}{7} \div \dfrac{2}{3} =$ _____

3. $\dfrac{9}{10} \div \dfrac{1}{2} =$ _____

4. $\dfrac{3}{4} \div \dfrac{2}{5} =$ _____

5. $\dfrac{2}{9} \div \dfrac{3}{12} =$ _____

6. $\dfrac{3}{8} \div \dfrac{4}{5} =$ _____

7. $\dfrac{5}{6} \div \dfrac{5}{6} =$ _____

8. $\dfrac{3}{10} \div \dfrac{4}{5} =$ _____

9. $\dfrac{5}{12} \div \dfrac{2}{3} =$ _____

10. $\dfrac{3}{5} \div \dfrac{7}{8} =$ _____

11. $\dfrac{3}{5} \div \dfrac{5}{6} =$ _____

12. $\dfrac{1}{2} \div \dfrac{1}{8} =$ _____

13. $\dfrac{1}{12} \div \dfrac{3}{15} =$ _____

14. $\dfrac{1}{15} \div \dfrac{3}{15} =$ _____

15. $\dfrac{3}{20} \div \dfrac{3}{5} =$ _____

16. $\dfrac{1}{8} \div \dfrac{5}{6} =$ _____

Apply

17. A bird feeder holds $\dfrac{1}{2}$ cup of birdseed. The feeder is filled with a scoop that holds $\dfrac{1}{6}$ of a cup. How many scoops will be needed to fill the feeder?

_____

18. Explain how you got the answer for problem 17. _____

_____

_____

_____

Lesson Introduction: Dividing Whole Numbers and Mixed Numbers

Common Core State Standard	Objective
• Fifth Grade: 5.NF.3, 5.NF.7 • Sixth Grade: 6.NS.1 • Seventh Grade: 7.NS.2, 7.NS.3 • Eighth Grade: 8.NS.1	• Divide a whole number by a mixed number. • Divide a mixed number by a whole number.

Vocabulary

convert, fraction, reciprocal, improper fraction, invert, mixed number, whole number

Overview

A **fraction** expresses a whole divided into any number of equal parts. It is a number usually expressed in the form a/b. A **whole number** is a counting number, such as 1, 2, or 3. A **mixed number** is a whole number and a fraction. A mixed number can be converted to an improper fraction. An **improper fraction** is a fraction in which the numerator is greater than the denominator. To **convert** means to change.

Dividing fractions requires using the reciprocal. One number is the **reciprocal** of another if their product is 1. When you turn the fraction upside down or **invert** the fraction, you have a reciprocal of the original fraction.

Dividing Whole Numbers and Mixed Numbers

Place the whole number over the denominator of 1. Convert the mixed number to an improper fraction. Invert the improper fraction and change the sign to multiplication. Convert the answer back to a mixed number.

$$14 \div 2\frac{1}{2} = \frac{14}{1} \div \frac{5}{2} = \frac{14}{1} \times \frac{2}{5} = \frac{28}{5} = 5\frac{3}{5}$$

Dividing Mixed Numbers

Convert the mixed numbers to improper fractions. Invert the second improper fraction and change the sign to multiplication. Simplify before multiplying, if possible. Convert the answer back to a mixed number.

$$3\frac{3}{5} \div 2\frac{2}{3} = \frac{18}{3} \div \frac{8}{3} = \frac{\overset{9}{\cancel{18}}}{\underset{1}{\cancel{3}}} \times \frac{\overset{1}{\cancel{3}}}{\underset{4}{\cancel{8}}} = \frac{9}{4} = 2\frac{1}{4}$$

Problems to Try

a. $4 \div 1\frac{1}{2} =$ Answer: $2\frac{2}{3}$

b. $5\frac{1}{4} \div 1\frac{3}{4} =$ Answer: 3

Real-World Connection

In U.S. currency, a penny is one-hundredth of a dollar, a nickel is one-twentieth of a dollar, a dime is one-tenth of a dollar, and a quarter is one-fourth of a dollar.

Name: _____   Date: _____

Practice: Dividing Whole Numbers and Mixed Numbers

Directions: Solve the problems below by dividing the mixed numbers and whole numbers. Simplify the answers.

1. $8 \div 1\frac{3}{5} =$ _____

2. $2\frac{1}{2} \div 8 =$ _____

3. $3\frac{3}{8} \div 9 =$ _____

4. $7 \div 3\frac{1}{2} =$ _____

5. $4\frac{1}{2} \div 1\frac{1}{2} =$ _____

6. $2\frac{1}{4} \div 1\frac{3}{4} =$ _____

7. $25 \div 3\frac{1}{8} =$ _____

8. $3\frac{1}{8} \div 4\frac{1}{2} =$ _____

9. $18 \div 1\frac{4}{5} =$ _____

10. $2\frac{1}{4} \div 2\frac{1}{2} =$ _____

11. $4\frac{1}{6} \div 1\frac{1}{3} =$ _____

12. $12 \div 2\frac{2}{3} =$ _____

13. $1\frac{2}{7} \div 5 =$ _____

14. $5\frac{5}{6} \div 7 =$ _____

15. $7\frac{1}{5} \div 1\frac{1}{5} =$ _____

16. $36 \div 1\frac{1}{2} =$ _____

Apply

17. Flood water is rising at $1\frac{1}{2}$ inches per hour. How many hours will it take the water to rise 12 inches? _____

18. Explain how you got the answer for problem 17. _____

_____

_____

_____

Name: _____   Date: _____

Unit Assessment: Dividing Fractions and Mixed Numbers

Directions: Fill in the bubble next to the correct answer for each multiple choice question.

1. What is the reciprocal of $\frac{5}{9}$?

    ○ **a.** $\frac{5}{9}$

    ○ **b.** $\frac{9}{5}$

    ○ **c.** $\frac{5}{6}$

    ○ **d.** $\frac{4}{9}$

4. What is the reciprocal of $6\frac{1}{3}$?

    ○ **a.** $\frac{19}{3}$

    ○ **b.** $\frac{10}{1}$

    ○ **c.** $\frac{3}{19}$

    ○ **d.** $\frac{10}{3}$

2. What is the reciprocal of 10?

    ○ **a.** $\frac{1}{10}$

    ○ **b.** $\frac{10}{3}$

    ○ **c.** $\frac{7}{10}$

    ○ **d.** $\frac{10}{1}$

5. $\frac{2}{3} \div \frac{1}{4} =$

    ○ **a.** $1\frac{2}{3}$

    ○ **b.** $2\frac{2}{3}$

    ○ **c.** $\frac{2}{12}$

    ○ **d.** $\frac{1}{6}$

3. What is the reciprocal of $5\frac{3}{4}$?

    ○ **a.** $\frac{23}{5}$

    ○ **b.** $\frac{23}{4}$

    ○ **c.** $\frac{12}{4}$

    ○ **d.** $\frac{4}{23}$

6. $\frac{3}{8} \div \frac{2}{7} =$

    ○ **a.** $1\frac{5}{16}$

    ○ **b.** $1\frac{1}{16}$

    ○ **c.** $\frac{3}{28}$

    ○ **d.** $2\frac{1}{16}$

Name: _____ Date: _____

Unit Assessment: Dividing Fractions and Mixed Numbers (cont.)

7. $7 \div \frac{2}{5} =$

   ○ **a.** $14\frac{1}{2}$

   ○ **b.** $17\frac{4}{5}$

   ○ **c.** $2\frac{4}{5}$

   ○ **d.** $17\frac{1}{2}$

10. $1\frac{2}{3} \div 2\frac{1}{4} =$

   ○ **a.** $\frac{20}{27}$

   ○ **b.** $2\frac{3}{4}$

   ○ **c.** $3\frac{3}{4}$

   ○ **d.** $\frac{1}{3}$

8. $\frac{1}{2} \div 3 =$

   ○ **a.** $1\frac{1}{2}$

   ○ **b.** $\frac{1}{8}$

   ○ **c.** $\frac{1}{6}$

   ○ **d.** $1\frac{1}{3}$

11. $5 \div \frac{5}{6} =$

   ○ **a.** $4\frac{1}{6}$

   ○ **b.** 6

   ○ **c.** $\frac{1}{6}$

   ○ **d.** $3\frac{1}{6}$

9. $\frac{2}{5} \div 4 =$

   ○ **a.** $\frac{1}{10}$

   ○ **b.** $1\frac{3}{5}$

   ○ **c.** $2\frac{1}{3}$

   ○ **d.** $\frac{9}{10}$

12. $2\frac{1}{3} \div 1\frac{1}{2} =$

   ○ **a.** $3\frac{1}{2}$

   ○ **b.** $2\frac{5}{9}$

   ○ **c.** $1\frac{5}{9}$

   ○ **d.** $1\frac{2}{9}$

Lesson Introduction: Converting Decimals to Fractions

Common Core State Standard	Objective
• Fifth Grade: 5.NBT.3 • Eighth Grade: 8.NS.1	• Convert decimals through thousandths to fractions.

Vocabulary
convert, decimal, decimal point, fraction

Overview
A **decimal** is a fractional number written after a period called a **decimal point**. A **fraction** expresses a whole divided into any number of equal parts. It is a number usually expressed in the form *a/b*. It is easy to **convert** or change a decimal to a fraction.

Converting Decimals to Fractions

Examples

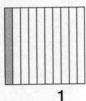

$0.1 = \dfrac{1}{10}$

If a whole is divided into 10 equal parts, each part is 1 tenth.

$0.15 = \dfrac{15}{100}$

If a whole is divided into 100 equal parts, each part is 1 hundredth.

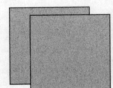

$2.4 = 2\dfrac{4}{10}$

The decimal point is read as *and* in numbers greater than 1.0. The decimal above is read as "two *and* four-tenths."

The place value of a decimal is determined by the number of digits to the right of the decimal point.

Decimal	Place Value	Words	Fraction Value
0.2	tenths	two-tenths	2/10
0.02	hundredths	two-hundredths	2/100
0.002	thousandths	two-thousandths	2/1000
0.0002	ten-thousandths	two ten-thousandths	2/10000

Problems to Try
Write the fraction for each decimal.

a. 0.3 **Answer:** $\dfrac{3}{10}$ **b.** 0.78 **Answer:** $\dfrac{78}{100}$ **c.** 0.0004 **Answer:** $\dfrac{4}{10000}$

d. 8.06 **Answer:** $8\dfrac{6}{100}$

Real-World Connection
A familiar use of decimals is with money. Examples of decimals as money are $0.47, $6.50, and $20.00.

Practice: Converting Decimals to Fractions

Directions: Write each decimal as a fraction or mixed number. Do not simplify.

1. 0.23 = _____

2. 0.06 = _____

3. 0.7 = _____

4. 0.013 = _____

5. 0.074 = _____

6. 0.88 = _____

7. 0.9 = _____

8. 0.034 = _____

9. 3.7 = _____

10. 18.08 = _____

11. 47.073 = _____

12. 17.5 = _____

13. 4.001 = _____

14. 5.62 = _____

15. 50.1 = _____

16. 36.19 = _____

Apply

17. Max walked 0.9 mile to the post office. What is the fraction for this decimal? _____

18. Diane paid $179.35 for a new bike. What is the fraction for this decimal? _____

Lesson Introduction: Converting Fractions to Decimals

Common Core State Standard	Objective
• Fifth Grade: 5.NBT.3 • Eighth Grade: 8.NS.1	• Convert fractions to decimals through thousandths.

Vocabulary
decimal, decimal point, fraction, convert

Overview
A **fraction** expresses a whole divided into any number of equal parts. It is a number usually expressed in the form a/b. A **decimal** is a fractional number written after a period called a **decimal point**. It is easy to **convert** or change a fraction to a decimal.

Converting Fractions to Decimals

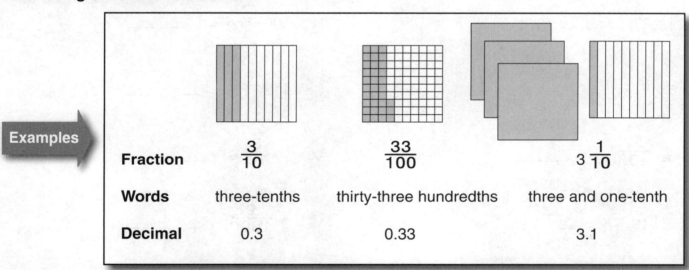

Examples

Fraction	$\frac{3}{10}$	$\frac{33}{100}$	$3\frac{1}{10}$
Words	three-tenths	thirty-three hundredths	three and one-tenth
Decimal	0.3	0.33	3.1

Problems to Try
Write the fraction for each decimal.

a. $\frac{5}{10}$ **Answer:** 0.5   b. $\frac{14}{100}$ **Answer:** 0.14

c. $\frac{198}{1000}$ **Answer:** 0.198   d. $25\frac{7}{100}$ **Answer:** 25.07

Real-World Connection

Map navigation systems give directions using decimals and fractions, such as "Go 7.9 ($7\frac{9}{10}$) miles."

Practice: Converting Fractions to Decimals

Directions: Write a decimal for each fraction or mixed number.

1. $\frac{1}{10}$ = _____

2. $\frac{37}{100}$ = _____

3. $\frac{8}{100}$ = _____

4. $\frac{3}{10}$ = _____

5. $7\frac{1}{100}$ = _____

6. $\frac{7}{1000}$ = _____

7. $13\frac{1}{10}$ = _____

8. $\frac{64}{1000}$ = _____

9. $\frac{17}{100}$ = _____

10. $47\frac{9}{10}$ = _____

11. $57\frac{84}{100}$ = _____

12. $506\frac{73}{1000}$ = _____

13. $112\frac{69}{100}$ = _____

14. $27\frac{3}{10}$ = _____

15. $9\frac{9}{1000}$ = _____

16. $2\frac{35}{100}$ = _____

Apply

17. What is the word form of 87.004? _____

18. What is the decimal for $93\frac{67}{100}$? _____

Lesson Introduction: Dividing to Convert Fractions to Decimals

Common Core State Standard	Objective
• Fifth Grade: 5.NBT.3, 5.NBT.4, 5.NBT.5, 5.NBT.7 • Sixth Grade: 6.NS.3 • Seventh Grade: 7.NS.2 • Eighth Grade: 8.NS.1	• Use division to express a fraction as a decimal.

Vocabulary

decimal, decimal point, denominator, fraction, numerator, quotient

Overview

A **fraction** expresses a whole divided into any number of equal parts. It is a number usually expressed in the form a/b. A **decimal** is a fractional number written after a period called a **decimal point**. Division can be used to express a fraction as a decimal. To express a fraction as a decimal, divide the **numerator** (top number) by the **denominator** (bottom number). The answer to a division problem is the **quotient**. The quotient is the decimal version of the fraction.

Dividing to Convert Fractions to Decimals

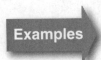

Examples

To express $\frac{1}{5}$ as a decimal, divide 1 by 5. Divide until the remainder is zero.

$$
\begin{array}{r}
0.2 \\
5 \overline{)1.0} \\
-10 \\
\hline
0
\end{array}
$$

To express $\frac{2}{3}$ as a decimal, divide 2 by 3. Divide until you can round the quotient to the nearest thousandth.

$$
\begin{array}{r}
0.6666 = 0.667 \\
3 \overline{)2.0000} \\
-18 \\
\hline
20 \\
-18 \\
\hline
20 \\
-18 \\
\hline
20 \\
-18 \\
\hline
2
\end{array}
$$

Problems to Try

a. Divide to express $\frac{3}{16}$ as a decimal. Continue dividing until the remainder is zero.

Answer: 0.1875

b. Divide to express $\frac{2}{9}$ as a decimal. Divide until you can round the quotient to the nearest thousandth.   **Answer:** 0.222

Real-World Connection

When you buy or sell anything in the United States, you are using decimals and fractions. A dime is 1/10 of a dollar or $0.10.

Name: _____   Date: _____

Practice: Dividing to Convert Fractions to Decimals

Directions: Write a decimal for each fraction. Divide until the remainder is zero.

1. $\dfrac{2}{5}$ = _____   **9.** $\dfrac{9}{16}$ = _____

2. $\dfrac{1}{8}$ = _____   **10.** $\dfrac{1}{5}$ = _____

3. $\dfrac{8}{100}$ = _____   **11.** $\dfrac{5}{8}$ = _____

4. $\dfrac{3}{4}$ = _____   **12.** $\dfrac{7}{8}$ = _____

5. $\dfrac{1}{2}$ = _____   **13.** $\dfrac{3}{8}$ = _____

6. $\dfrac{3}{5}$ = _____   **14.** $\dfrac{4}{5}$ = _____

7. $\dfrac{1}{4}$ = _____   **15.** $\dfrac{3}{50}$ = _____

8. $\dfrac{9}{20}$ = _____   **16.** $\dfrac{7}{16}$ = _____

Apply

17. The music store is having a $\dfrac{1}{4}$ off special on all CDs. What is this fraction written as a decimal? _____

18. $\dfrac{3}{5}$ of Miss Craig's class are girls. What is this fraction written as a decimal? _____

Name: _____ Date: _____

Unit Assessment: Fractions and Decimals

Directions: Fill in the bubble next to the correct answer for each multiple choice question.

1. What is the fraction for 0.007?

○ **a.** $\frac{7}{100}$

○ **b.** $\frac{700}{1000}$

○ **c.** $\frac{70}{100}$

○ **d.** $\frac{7}{1000}$

2. What is the fraction for 0.61?

○ **a.** $\frac{61}{100}$

○ **b.** $\frac{61}{10}$

○ **c.** $\frac{61}{1000}$

○ **d.** $\frac{16}{1000}$

3. What is the fraction for 16.57?

○ **a.** $6\frac{57}{100}$

○ **b.** $16\frac{57}{1000}$

○ **c.** $61\frac{57}{100}$

○ **d.** $16\frac{57}{100}$

4. What is the fraction for 83.097?

○ **a.** $83\frac{97}{100}$

○ **b.** $83\frac{97}{1000}$

○ **c.** $38\frac{97}{1000}$

○ **d.** $830\frac{97}{1000}$

5. What is the decimal for $\frac{3}{100}$?

○ **a.** 0.30

○ **b.** 0.03

○ **c.** 0.003

○ **d.** 0.33

6. What is the decimal for $8\frac{7}{1000}$?

○ **a.** 0.007

○ **b.** 8.07

○ **c.** 8.007

○ **d.** 8.7

Name: _____ Date: _____

Unit Assessment: Fractions and Decimals (cont.)

7. What is the decimal for $25\frac{7}{10}$?

- ○ **a.** 25.7
- ○ **b.** 25.07
- ○ **c.** 25.007
- ○ **d.** 25.17

8. What is the decimal for $506\frac{73}{1000}$?

- ○ **a.** 516.073
- ○ **b.** 506.173
- ○ **c.** 506.730
- ○ **d.** 506.073

9. What is the decimal for $\frac{1}{4}$?

- ○ **a.** 0.5
- ○ **b.** 0.75
- ○ **c.** 0.25
- ○ **d.** 0.35

10. What is the decimal for $\frac{7}{8}$?

- ○ **a.** 0.587
- ○ **b.** 1.14
- ○ **c.** 0.875
- ○ **d.** 0.785

11. What is the decimal for $\frac{3}{8}$?

- ○ **a.** 0.475
- ○ **b.** 0.375
- ○ **c.** 0.655
- ○ **d.** 0.575

12. What is the decimal for $\frac{3}{50}$?

- ○ **a.** 0.060
- ○ **b.** 0.075
- ○ **c.** 0.083
- ○ **d.** 0.036

Lesson Introduction: Converting Fractions to Percents

Common Core State Standard	Objective
• Fifth Grade: 5.NF.3 • Sixth Grade: 6.RP.3 • Seventh Grade: 7.RP.3 • Eighth Grade: 8.NS.1	• Convert a fraction to a percent.

Vocabulary

convert, fraction, percent

Overview

Fractions and percents are basically the same thing—both represent "parts of a whole" or "a part of." A **fraction** expresses a whole divided into any number of equal parts. It is a number usually expressed in the form a/b. **Percent** means hundredths or out of 100. The symbol for percent is %. It is easy to convert fractions to percents. **Convert** means to change.

Converting Fractions to Percents

Examples

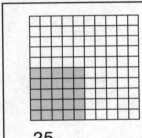

$\frac{25}{100}$ is shaded

$\frac{25}{100} = 25\%$

You can write a cross-product problem to find a percent. Remember, percent means hundredths.

$\frac{4}{5}$ is what percent?

Write the cross-products.   Divide.

$$\frac{n}{100} = \frac{4}{5} = \frac{100 \times 4}{n \times 5} = 5\overline{\smash)400}\;^{80\%}$$

Write the answer.

Problems to Try

a. Write a percent for $\frac{75}{100}$.   **Answer:** 75%

b. Write a percent for $\frac{1}{5}$.   **Answer:** 20%

c. 53 of the 100 students are girls. What percent are girls?   **Answer:** 53%

Real-World Connection

Most states have a sales tax. This is a tax paid by the consumer when they buy something. Sales tax on a new car can amount to more than most people expect. An 8% sales tax on a soda isn't too much, but 8% on a $40,000 car will cost you $3,200!

Practice: Converting Fractions to Percents

Directions: Write a percent for each fraction.

1. $\dfrac{15}{100}$ = _____

2. $\dfrac{29}{100}$ = _____

3. $\dfrac{8}{100}$ = _____

4. $\dfrac{1}{100}$ = _____

5. $\dfrac{62}{100}$ = _____

6. $\dfrac{99}{100}$ = _____

7. $\dfrac{13}{100}$ = _____

8. $\dfrac{56}{100}$ = _____

9. $\dfrac{2}{5}$ = _____

10. $\dfrac{1}{4}$ = _____

11. $\dfrac{1}{2}$ = _____

12. $\dfrac{3}{4}$ = _____

13. $\dfrac{3}{5}$ = _____

14. $\dfrac{4}{25}$ = _____

15. $\dfrac{9}{20}$ = _____

16. $\dfrac{17}{50}$ = _____

Apply

17. 88 of the 100 students like to play video games. What percent do not? _____

18. The bike shop has 100 bikes for sale. 45 of the bikes are red. What percent are red?

    _____

Lesson Introduction: Probability

Common Core State Standard	Objective
• Fifth Grade: 5.NF.3, 5.NF.4, 5.NF.6 • Sixth Grade: 6.NS.1, 6.PR.1 • Seventh Grade: 7.NS.2, 7.NS.3, 7.SP.5-7 • Eighth Grade: 8.NS.1	• Use a fraction to express probability.

Vocabulary

probability

Overview

Probability is the chance or likelihood that an event will happen. The probability of an event happening can be written as a fraction.

$$\text{Probability of an event occurring} = \frac{\text{Number of ways it can happen}}{\text{Total number of possible outcomes}}$$

Probability

Examples →

If you toss a coin, there are two possible outcomes: heads or tails.

- • The probability of a coin landing head side up is $\frac{1}{2}$.
- • The probability of a coin landing tail side up is $\frac{1}{2}$.

There are 42 marbles in the bag.

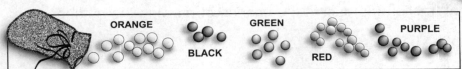

- • The probability of drawing an orange marble from the bag is $\frac{11}{42}$.
- • The probability of drawing a red marble from the bag is $\frac{12}{42}$.

$\frac{12}{42}$ simplified is $\frac{2}{7}$.

Problems to Try

a. If you toss a coin 100 times, how many times will heads come up?   **Answer:** 50

b. What is the probability of drawing a green marble from the bag of marbles above?

Answer: $\frac{1}{7}$

Real-World Connection

The population of the United States is about 310 million. In the United States, an average of 40 people are killed by lightning each year. The chance of being killed by lightning in the United States is equal to 40/310 million.

Name: _____ Date: _____

Practice: Probability

Directions: Use the spinner to answer questions 1 through 3. Simplify the fractions.

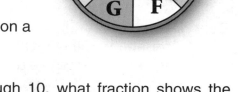

1. What fraction represents the chance of the spinner landing on a D? _____

2. What fraction represents the chance of the spinner landing on a vowel? _____

3. What fraction represents the chance of the spinner landing on a consonant? _____

4. On a spinner divided into 10 equal parts labeled 1 through 10, what fraction shows the chance of the spinner landing on an even number? _____

Directions: Use the bag of numbers to answer questions 5 through 7. Simplify the fractions.

5. What fraction represents the chance of drawing the number 19 from the bag? _____

6. What fraction represents the chance of drawing the number 4 from the bag? _____

7. What fraction represents the chance of drawing the number 13 from the bag? _____

Directions: Use the spinner to answer questions 8 through 10. Simplify the fractions.

8. What fraction of the spinner is shaded? _____

9. About what fraction of the spins can you expect to stop on the shaded section of the spinner? _____

10. About how many times would you expect to stop on the shaded section if you made 60 spins? _____

Lesson Introduction: Meaning of Ratios

Common Core State Standard	Objective
• Fifth Grade: 5.NBT.3 • Sixth Grade: 6.RP.1-3 • Seventh Grade: 7.SP.1-3 • Eighth Grade: 8.NS.1	• Describe ratios with numbers.

Vocabulary

ratio, rate, expressed

Overview

A **ratio** is a pair of numbers that expresses a rate or comparison. It is a comparison of the size of one number to the size of another number. A **rate** is a ratio that expresses how long it takes to do something, such as traveling a certain distance. Ratios can be **expressed** or written in different ways.

Writing Ratios

Examples

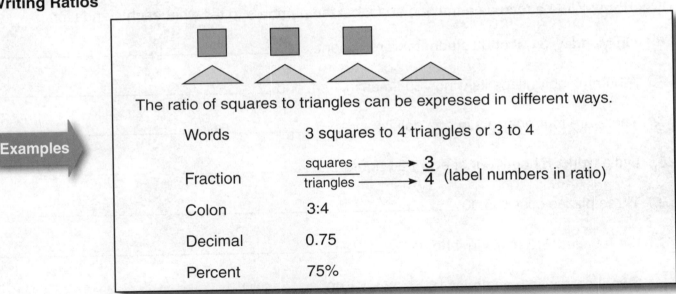

The ratio of squares to triangles can be expressed in different ways.

Words	3 squares to 4 triangles or 3 to 4
Fraction	$\dfrac{\text{squares}}{\text{triangles}} \longrightarrow \dfrac{3}{4}$ (label numbers in ratio)
Colon	3:4
Decimal	0.75
Percent	75%

Problems to Try

Write a ratio expressing the number of squares to circles as a fraction (label numbers), decimal, and percent.

Answer: $\dfrac{\text{squares}}{\text{circles}} \longrightarrow \dfrac{1}{3}$, 0.33, 33%

Real-World Connection

Pharmacists must be familiar with ratios and rates. Prescription dosages are based on a ratio of medicine to body mass and to frequency of ingestion.

Practice: Meaning of Ratios

Directions: Use the triangle and circles to answer questions 1–4.

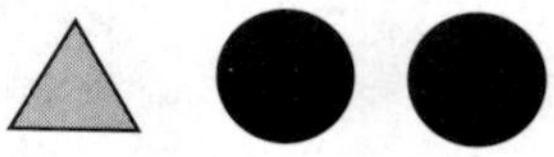

1. Write a ratio expressing the number of triangles to circles as a fraction.

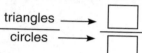

2. Write a ratio expressing the number of triangles to circles using a colon.

3. Write a ratio expressing the number of triangles to circles as a decimal.

4. Write a ratio expressing the number of triangles to circles as a percent.

Directions: Write a ratio as a fraction and label the numbers to tell what each stands for.

5. On Monday, 3 out of 30 students were absent.

6. A hummingbird flaps its wings 60 times in 1 second.

7. There are four quarters in one dollar.

8. Lydia works 8 hours out of every 24 hours.

9. Three pizzas cost $15.00.

10. We traveled 213 miles in 4 hours.

11. Sweet corn was on sale for 10 ears for $1.00.

12. Marie swims 8 strokes in 5 meters.

13. Kris does two push-ups in three seconds.

14. There are two cups of tomato sauce in each can.

15. There are 16 cups of milk in each gallon.

16. Canned green beans are on sale for 6 cans for 79¢.

Header: Multiplying and Dividing Fractions — Name: — Date: — Meaning of Ratios

Lesson Introduction: Finding Equivalent Ratios

Common Core State Standard	Objective
• Fifth Grade: 5.NBT.3 • Sixth Grade: 6.RP.1-3 • Seventh Grade: 7.SP.1-3 • Eighth Grade: 8.NS.1	• Write a ratio and label the numbers. • Use multiplication to find equivalent ratios.

Vocabulary
ratio, rate, equivalent

Overview
A **ratio** is a pair of numbers that expresses a rate or comparison. It is a comparison of the size of one number to the size of another number. A **rate** is a ratio that expresses how long it takes to do something, such as traveling a certain distance. **Equivalent** ratios are ratios that are equal.

Finding Equivalent Ratios

Examples

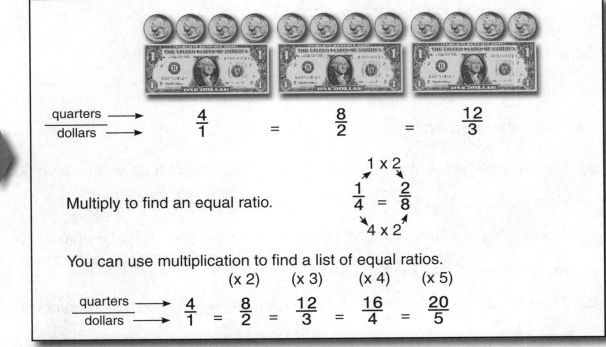

quarters →
dollars →
$$\frac{4}{1} = \frac{8}{2} = \frac{12}{3}$$

Multiply to find an equal ratio.

$$\overset{1 \times 2}{\frac{1}{4}} = \underset{4 \times 2}{\frac{2}{8}}$$

You can use multiplication to find a list of equal ratios.

$$\quad\quad (\times 2) \quad (\times 3) \quad (\times 4) \quad (\times 5)$$

quarters →
dollars →
$$\frac{4}{1} = \frac{8}{2} = \frac{12}{3} = \frac{16}{4} = \frac{20}{5}$$

Problems to Try
The team scored 4 goals in 7 games. List equal ratios to find how many goals the team will score in 42 soccer games.

Answer: goals → games →
$$\frac{4}{7} = \frac{8}{14} = \frac{12}{21} = \frac{16}{28} = \frac{20}{35} = \frac{24}{42}$$

Real-World Connection
Ratios are important in education. Research suggests that low student-to-teacher ratios promote higher achievement levels. A 15:1 student-to-teacher ratio is better than a 25:1 ratio.

Name: _____ Date: _____

Practice: Finding Equivalent Ratios

Directions: Multiply to complete the list of equal ratios.

1. Home runs: 2 home runs to 1 game

$$\frac{\text{home runs}}{\text{games}} = \frac{2}{1} = \underline{\quad} = \underline{\quad} = \underline{\quad} = \underline{\quad} = \underline{\quad}$$

2. Pets in homes: 5 dogs to 3 cats

$$\frac{\text{dogs}}{\text{cats}} = \frac{5}{3} = \underline{\quad} = \underline{\quad} = \underline{\quad} = \underline{\quad} = \underline{\quad}$$

3. Shoe sale: 2 pair shoes to $25.00

$$\frac{\text{pairs of shoes}}{\text{dollars}} = \frac{2}{\$25.00} = \underline{\quad} = \underline{\quad} = \underline{\quad} = \underline{\quad} = \underline{\quad}$$

4. Computers: 3 computers to 15 students

$$\frac{\text{computers}}{\text{students}} = \frac{3}{15} = \underline{\quad} = \underline{\quad} = \underline{\quad} = \underline{\quad} = \underline{\quad}$$

5. Meters run: 45 meters to 9 seconds

$$\frac{\text{meters}}{\text{seconds}} = \frac{45}{9} = \underline{\quad} = \underline{\quad} = \underline{\quad} = \underline{\quad} = \underline{\quad}$$

Direction: Solve each problem.

6. It takes 9 players to make a team. How many teams can be formed from 63 players? _____

7. The pitching machine throws 25 baseballs in 12 minutes. How many baseballs will it throw in 60 minutes? _____

8. There are 6 pieces of pie in each pan. How many pies do you need to serve 48 people? _____

9. Jason can do 7 sit-ups in 8 seconds. How may sit-ups can he do in 56 seconds? _____

10. Lori got 3 hits for every 8 times at bat. How many hits will she get every 24 times at bat? _____

Lesson Introduction: Finding Missing Numbers and Cross-Products of Ratios

Common Core State Standard	Objective
• Fifth Grade: 5.NBT.3 • Sixth Grade: 6.RP.1-3 • Seventh Grade: 7.SP.1-3 • Eighth Grade: 8.NS.1	• Find the missing number in a ratio. • Cross multiply to find if two ratios are equal.

Vocabulary
> equivalent, rate, ratio

Overview
> A **ratio** is a pair of numbers that expresses a rate or comparison. It is a comparison of the size of one number to the size of another number. A **rate** is a ratio that expresses how long it takes to do something, such as traveling a certain distance. **Equivalent** ratios are ratios that are equal.

Finding Missing Numbers

Example

Find n in $\dfrac{1}{4} = \dfrac{n}{8}$

$n = 2$

How many times does 4 divide into 8? Multiply that number times the numerator 1.

$$\overset{1 \times 2}{\dfrac{1}{4}} = \underset{4 \times 2}{\dfrac{2}{8}}$$

Cross-Product of Ratios

Example

Cross multiply to find if two ratios are equal.

$$\dfrac{2}{3} \bowtie \dfrac{6}{9} = \dfrac{18}{18}$$

The two ratios are equivalent because their cross-products are the same.

Problems to Try

a. Find n for the ratio.

$\dfrac{3}{9} = \dfrac{6}{n}$ **Answer:** 18

b. Marilyn uses 3 eggs to make 4 slices of French toast. How many eggs will she use for 12 slices of French toast?
Answer: 9

c. Are the ratios $\dfrac{3}{4}$ and $\dfrac{6}{8}$ equal? Find the cross-products to help you decide.
Answer: yes

Real-World Connection
> Jobs in the medical field involve using equipment to measure ratios and rates such as blood pressure and pulse.

Name: _____   Date: _____

Practice: Finding Missing Numbers and Cross-Products of Ratios

Directions: Find *n* in each problem below.

Directions: Tell whether the ratios are equal. Find the cross-products to help you decide.

1. $\frac{1}{6} = \frac{n}{30}$ n = _____

2. $\frac{5}{8} = \frac{20}{n}$ n = _____

3. $\frac{1}{2} = \frac{5}{n}$ n = _____

4. $\frac{4}{6} = \frac{n}{24}$ n = _____

5. $\frac{1}{3} = \frac{3}{n}$ n = _____

6. $\frac{1}{4} = \frac{2}{n}$ n = _____

7. $\frac{2}{3} = \frac{n}{15}$ n = _____

8. $\frac{1}{2}$ $\frac{3}{4}$ yes   no

9. $\frac{2}{3}$ $\frac{5}{6}$ yes   no

10. $\frac{2}{5}$ $\frac{4}{10}$ yes   no

11. $\frac{7}{8}$ $\frac{3}{6}$ yes   no

12. $\frac{2}{6}$ $\frac{3}{9}$ yes   no

13. $\frac{1}{2}$ $\frac{5}{15}$ yes   no

14. $\frac{2}{3}$ $\frac{7}{8}$ yes   no

Apply

15. A boat travels 780 kilometers in 2 hours. How many kilometers will it travel in 8 hours?

_____

16. A car travels 26 kilometers in 3 minutes. How many kilometers will it travel in 15 minutes?_____

17. Sam drinks 3 glasses of orange juice in one week. How many glasses of juice does he drink in 5 weeks? _____

Name: _____   Date: _____

Unit Assessment: Percents/Probability/Ratios

Directions: Fill in the bubble next to the correct answer for each multiple choice question.

1. What is the percent for $\frac{27}{100}$?

   ○ **a.** 25%

   ○ **b.** 32%

   ○ **c.** 27%

   ○ **d.** 85%

2. What is the percent for $\frac{4}{5}$?

   ○ **a.** 20%

   ○ **b.** 65%

   ○ **c.** 74%

   ○ **d.** 80%

3. What is the percent for $\frac{9}{10}$?

   ○ **a.** 9%

   ○ **b.** 90%

   ○ **c.** 0.09%

   ○ **d.** 19%

4. If you toss a coin 30 times, how many times is tails likely to come up?

   ○ **a.** 30

   ○ **b.** 10

   ○ **c.** 15

   ○ **d.** 3

5. There are 21 marbles in a bag. Seven of the marbles are black. What is the probability of drawing a black marble?

   ○ **a.** $\frac{2}{3}$

   ○ **b.** $\frac{7}{20}$

   ○ **c.** $\frac{1}{3}$

   ○ **d.** $\frac{21}{7}$

6.

What is the ratio that expresses the number of diamonds to ovals as a fraction?

   ○ **a.** $\frac{\text{circles}}{\text{squares}} = \frac{1}{3}$

   ○ **b.** $\frac{\text{ovals}}{\text{diamonds}} = \frac{1}{3}$

   ○ **c.** $\frac{\text{triangles}}{\text{circles}} = \frac{1}{3}$

   ○ **d.** $\frac{\text{diamonds}}{\text{ovals}} = \frac{1}{3}$

Name: _____ Date: _____

Unit Assessment: Percents/Probability/Ratios (cont.)

7.

What is the ratio expressing the number of diamonds to ovals using a colon?

○ **a.** 1:2

○ **b.** 2:1

○ **c.** 1:1

○ **d.** 2:2

8. What are the equivalent ratios for pets in homes: 2 dogs to 1 cat?

○ **a.** $\frac{dogs}{cats} = \frac{2}{1} = \frac{4}{2} = \frac{6}{3} = \frac{8}{4} = \frac{10}{5}$

○ **b.** $\frac{cats}{dogs} = \frac{2}{1} = \frac{4}{2} = \frac{6}{3} = \frac{8}{4} = \frac{10}{5}$

○ **c.** $\frac{dogs}{cats} = \frac{2}{1} = \frac{6}{2} = \frac{8}{3} = \frac{10}{4} = \frac{12}{5}$

○ **d.** $\frac{cats}{dogs} = \frac{2}{1} = \frac{6}{2} = \frac{8}{3} = \frac{10}{4} = \frac{12}{5}$

9. There are six candy bars in a package. How many packages do you need to serve 54 people?

○ **a.** 7 packages

○ **b.** 9 packages

○ **c.** 10 packages

○ **d.** 8 packages

10. What does n equal? $\frac{5}{8} = \frac{10}{n}$

○ **a.** 20

○ **b.** 18

○ **c.** 15

○ **d.** 16

11. What does n equal? $\frac{4}{6} = \frac{n}{36}$

○ **a.** 12

○ **b.** 24

○ **c.** 16

○ **d.** 22

12. A horseback rider travels 24 miles per day. How far can the rider travel in four days?

○ **a.** 69 miles

○ **b.** 96 miles

○ **c.** 106 miles

○ **d.** 86 miles

Learning Stations Activity: Teacher Page

Title: Exploring Fractions

Goal: To provide an opportunity for students to apply fractional skills and concepts.

Materials List/Setup

Station 1:   Fraction Cards: Eight cards with one letter of the word F R A C T I O N written on each card (These can be one-half or one-fourth of an index card.), Station One: Probability worksheet, one copy per student

Station 2:   Station Two: Take a Poll worksheet, one copy per student

Station 3:   Station Three: Sugar Cookie Recipe worksheet, one copy per student

Station 4:   Colored pencils or marking pens, Station Four: Using Pictures to Multiply Fractions worksheet, one copy per student

Opening: Discussion Questions

Real-World Application: Are there times you have used or encountered fractions outside of school? What occupations require an employee to understand and use fractions?

Student Instructions

The learning stations will give you the opportunity to apply what you know about fractions. You will be working in small groups to complete the worksheet for each station. Before moving to the next station, compare and discuss your answers with the group.

Closure: Reflection Questions

The following questions can be used to stimulate discussion or as a journaling activity.

1.   How can understanding fractions make your life easier?

2.   What is the role of fractions in mathematics? (Fractions are used for expressing both portions of a whole and portions of a group.)

Name: _____ Date: _____

Station One: Probability

Directions: Place the cards face down. Mix them up. Draw a card. Record the letter drawn with a tally mark in the table below. Replace the card. Mix up the cards again. After you have drawn, recorded, and tallied the draws 40 times, write a fraction and percent to represent the tally for each letter.

Outcome	Tally	Fraction	Percent
F			
R			
A			
C			
T			
I			
O			
N			

1. What fraction of the letters are vowels (a, e, i, o, u)? _____

2. What number of draws would you expect to be vowels if you make

    a. 8 draws? _____   **b.** 32 draws? _____

    c. 80 draws? _____   **d.** 96 draws? _____

Name: _____ Date: _____

Station Two: Take a Poll

Directions: Take a poll of the members of your group and fill in the chart below. Then answer the questions.

Eye Color	Girls	Boys
Blue		
Green		
Brown		
Other		

1. How many students are in your group? _____
2. What fraction of the girls have blue eyes? _____
3. What fraction of the group has brown eyes? _____
4. What fraction of the boys have green eyes? _____
5. Which fraction is greater, boys with blue eyes or girls with brown eyes? _____

Directions: Take another poll using three other options. Fill in the chart below.

	Girls	Boys

Directions: Write three different statements using fractions that come from the data in your table.

Example: $\frac{1}{2}$ of the girls like volleyball.

1. _____
2. _____
3. _____

Station Three: Sugar Cookie Recipe

Directions: Below is a list of the ingredients and amounts needed to make sugar cookies. You need to triple the recipe to make enough cookies for the school bake sale. Fill in the table with your answers in simplest form.

Sugar Cookies

$1\frac{1}{2}$ cups butter

2 cups sugar

4 eggs

$\frac{3}{4}$ teaspoon baking powder

$1\frac{1}{4}$ cups flour

$\frac{1}{4}$ teaspoon salt

Ingredient	Amount
1. Butter	
2. Sugar	
3. Eggs	
4. Baking Powder	
5. Flour	
6. Salt	

Directions: Use the recipe and table to answer the questions below.

7. To convert the recipe, which operation did you use? Explain. _____

_____

8. What is the ratio of cups of sugar to eggs in the recipe? _____

9. What is the ratio of baking powder to salt? _____

10. How much salt would be needed for 5 batches of sugar cookies? _____

11. Your friend says you need 1 teaspoon of salt for 5 batches of sugar cookies. Use complete sentences to explain what mistake he made in calculating his answer. _____

_____

_____

Name: _____   Date: _____

Station Four: Using Pictures to Multiply Fractions

Directions: You can draw a picture to help you multiply fractions.

Example: $\frac{1}{2}$ of $\frac{1}{4}$

First shade $\frac{1}{4}$.

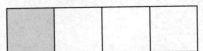

Next shade $\frac{1}{2}$ of that.

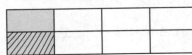

$\frac{1}{2}$ of $\frac{1}{4} = \frac{1}{8}$ or $\frac{1}{2} \times \frac{1}{4} = \frac{1}{8}$

Directions: Use the pictures to find the products.

1. $\frac{1}{4}$ of $\frac{1}{3}$ = _____

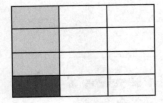

2. $\frac{2}{3}$ of $\frac{1}{6}$ = _____

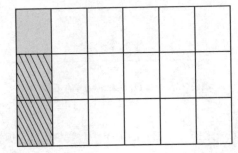

Directions: Draw a picture to help you find the products.

3. $\frac{2}{3}$ of $\frac{2}{5}$ = _____

4. $\frac{3}{4}$ of $\frac{2}{5}$ = _____

5. $\frac{3}{4}$ of $\frac{1}{3}$ = _____

6. $\frac{5}{6}$ of $\frac{1}{2}$ = _____

Daily Math Review

Daily Math Review #1

1. A tomato that weighed $3\frac{1}{4}$ pounds won the contest at the fair. How many ounces did it weigh? _____

2. Write $\frac{4}{32}$ as a decimal. _____

3. What is the greatest common factor of 8 and 36? _____

4. $\frac{3}{4} \times \frac{2}{5} =$ _____

5. $4 \div \frac{2}{7} =$ _____

Daily Math Review #2

1. A banner 40 ft. long was torn in the wind, and the last $\frac{1}{4}$ section of it blew away. How many feet of the banner was lost?

_____

2. Which is greater, 0.64 or $\frac{63}{100}$? _____

3. The player made 25 baskets in 12 minutes. How many baskets will she make in 60 minutes? _____

4. $\frac{3}{8} \times \frac{3}{8} =$ _____

5. $2\frac{3}{4} \div \frac{3}{8} =$ _____

Daily Math Review #3

1. The trout in a hatchery tank all weigh nearly $\frac{4}{5}$ of a pound. If there are 2,000 trout in this tank, about how many pounds of fish is that? _____

2. Write $\frac{3}{4}$ as a decimal. _____

3. Find the reciprocal of $7\frac{2}{5}$. _____

4. $1\frac{1}{9} \times 7 =$ _____

5. $6\frac{1}{4} \div \frac{3}{4} =$ _____

Daily Math Review #4

1. Steak is priced at $7.50 a pound. What would be the price of a steak that weighs $1\frac{1}{8}$ pounds? _____

2. Write $\frac{1}{3}$ as a decimal. Round the quotient to the nearest thousandth. _____

3. Find n in the ratio: $\frac{7}{9} = \frac{21}{n}$

_____

4. $2\frac{5}{6} \times \frac{8}{9} =$ _____

5. $2\frac{1}{3} \div \frac{7}{10} =$ _____

Daily Math Review

Daily Math Review #5

1. Dale bought $10\frac{4}{5}$ gallons of gasoline at a cost of $2.90 per gallon. How much was his total purchase? _____

2. Write the fraction for twenty-one-hundredths. _____

3. Find the reciprocal of $\frac{9}{12}$. _____

4. $\frac{6}{7} \times \frac{5}{12} =$ _____

5. $7\frac{1}{2} \div \frac{3}{4} =$ _____

Daily Math Review #6

1. A four-foot piece of string has been cut into five equal lengths. How long is each piece of string in inches? _____

2. Write the mixed number for 4.36. _____

3. Find n in the ratio: $\frac{6}{7} = \frac{n}{42}$ _____

4. $\frac{7}{12} \times \frac{4}{9} =$ _____

5. $4\frac{1}{6} \div 5 =$ _____

Daily Math Review #7

1. If an average milk cow can give $7\frac{2}{3}$ gallons of milk per day, how much milk should a herd of 40 cows produce in a day? _____

2. Write $\frac{7}{10}$ as a decimal. _____

3. Write a percent for $\frac{25}{100}$. _____

4. $\frac{2}{3} \times 16 =$ _____

5. $7\frac{1}{5} \div 1\frac{1}{6} =$ _____

Daily Math Review #8

1. A landowner with 2,100 acres of land splits this property equally among his six children. How much land will each child receive? _____

2. Write 22.05 as a fraction. _____

3. Write a percent for $\frac{3}{5}$. _____

4. $\frac{2}{5} \times 2\frac{1}{2} =$ _____

5. $15 \div 2\frac{3}{4} =$ _____

Daily Math Review

Daily Math Review #9

1. Janice bought $2\frac{3}{4}$ pounds of ground beef and made it into nine hamburgers. How many ounces did each hamburger weigh? _____

2. Find n in the ratio: $\frac{2}{3} = \frac{n}{6}$

_____

3. Find the reciprocal of $3\frac{3}{4}$. _____

4. $\frac{3}{8} \times \frac{7}{10} = $ _____

5. $3\frac{1}{4} \div 2 = $ _____

Daily Math Review #10

1. $\frac{2}{9}$ of the 18 students in a class have red hair. How many have red hair?

_____

2. What is the greatest common factor of 12 and 30? _____

3. Write a percent for $\frac{1}{5}$. _____

4. $1\frac{1}{4} \times 60 = $ _____

5. $5\frac{1}{4} \div \frac{3}{4} = $ _____

Daily Math Review #11

1. The Spanish Club had 30 members. Write a fraction to describe 18 who wanted to go on a trip to Mexico.

_____

2. Randy wants to make a 20-foot path of stepping stones. Each stone is $\frac{10}{12}$ of a foot long. How many stepping stones will he need? _____

3. Write the mixed number for 5.25.

_____

4. $1\frac{5}{6} \times 2\frac{1}{4} = $ _____

5. $6\frac{1}{2} \div 2\frac{1}{3} = $ _____

Daily Math Review #12

1. Of the town's 42 firefighters, 16 volunteered for the special rescue team. Express the portion who did not volunteer as a ratio. _____

2. Find n in the ratio: $\frac{1}{2} = \frac{6}{n}$.

_____

3. Find the reciprocal of $\frac{6}{9}$. _____

4. $1\frac{7}{8} \times 2\frac{1}{7} = $ _____

5. $8\frac{1}{6} \div 2\frac{1}{8} = $ _____

Daily Math Review

Daily Math Review #13

1. A can of dog food is $22\frac{3}{4}$ ounces. Each can contains $3\frac{1}{2}$ servings. How many ounces are in a serving? _____

2. Find n in the ratio: $\frac{4}{3} = \frac{32}{n}$

_____

3. Dominic can swim 9 strokes in 6 meters. Write a ratio as a fraction and label the numbers.

_____

4. $\frac{1}{2} \times \frac{2}{3} \times \frac{3}{4} =$ _____

5. $16 \div 2\frac{1}{2} =$ _____

Daily Math Review #14

1. Larry is 24. His brother is $\frac{2}{3}$ as old. How old is Larry's brother? _____

2. Three horses eat two bales of hay per day. Multiply to complete the list of equal ratios.

$$\frac{bales}{days} = \frac{2}{1} = \rule{1.5cm}{0.4pt} = \rule{1.5cm}{0.4pt} = \rule{1.5cm}{0.4pt}$$

3. Find the reciprocal of $7\frac{1}{8}$. _____

4. $\frac{5}{8} \times \frac{7}{10} \times \frac{4}{7} =$ _____

5. $64 \div 1\frac{3}{4} =$ _____

Daily Math Review #15

1. If one serving of cereal is $1\frac{1}{4}$ ounces, how many servings would be in a 10-ounce box of cereal? _____

2. Write three more equal ratios in the list.

$$\frac{3}{5} = \rule{1.5cm}{0.4pt} = \rule{1.5cm}{0.4pt} = \rule{1.5cm}{0.4pt}$$

3. Write a decimal for $\frac{3}{100}$. _____

4. $6\frac{7}{8} \times \frac{2}{11} \times \frac{4}{5} =$ _____

5. $5\frac{1}{2} \div 1\frac{1}{2} =$ _____

Daily Math Review #16

1. Jake and Zach ate $\frac{5}{6}$ of a dozen donuts. How many donuts are left?

_____

2. Write the word form of $2\frac{3}{5}$.

_____

3. Is the ratio equal? $\frac{3}{8}$ $\frac{6}{15}$

_____

4. $3\frac{1}{8} \times 7\frac{1}{5} \times 5\frac{1}{3} =$ _____

5. $14 \div \frac{7}{8} =$ _____

Glossary of Terms

common factor: a factor of two or more numbers that is the same; a common factor of 9 and 12 is 3.

convert: to change

cross-cancel: a method of simplifying before multiplying

decimal: a fractional number written after a period called a decimal point

decimal point: a period written before a fractional number

denominator: the bottom number of a fraction

divisor: a number used to divide another number

equivalent fractions: equal fractions; $\frac{2}{8}$ and $\frac{1}{4}$ are equivalent.

express: to write in a different way

factors: a number that divides another number evenly; the factors of 12 are 1, 2, 3, 4, 6, and 12.

fraction: a whole divided into any number of equal parts; a number usually expressed in the form a/b, such as $\frac{1}{2}$, $\frac{1}{3}$, or $\frac{1}{4}$

fraction bar: a line separating the numerator and denominator of a fraction; to divide

greatest common factor (GCF): the largest common factor of two or more numbers

improper fraction: a fraction in which the numerator is greater than the denominator, as in $\frac{7}{3}$, $\frac{10}{9}$, or $\frac{15}{6}$

mixed number: a whole number and a fraction, such as $3\frac{1}{2}$, $2\frac{1}{4}$, or $5\frac{3}{4}$

numerator: the top number of a fraction

percent: means hundredths or out of 100; the symbol for percent is %.

probability: the chance or likelihood that an event will happen

proper fraction: a fraction in which the numerator is less than the denominator, as in $\frac{1}{2}$, $\frac{2}{3}$, or $\frac{3}{4}$.

quotient: the answer in a division problem; 8 is the quotient in the problem: $48 \div 6 = 8$

rate: a ratio that expresses how long it takes to do something, such as traveling a distance

ratio: a pair of numbers that expresses a rate or comparison

reciprocal: two numbers whose product is 1; the reciprocal of $\frac{3}{4}$ is $\frac{4}{3}$ since $\frac{3}{4} \times \frac{4}{3} = 1$.

remainder: an amount left over when one number is divided by another number; when 10 is divided by 3, the remainder is 1.

rename: to change

simplify: to rewrite the answer in its lowest term

standard form: to write as a number; the standard form of three and one-half is $3\frac{1}{2}$.

whole number: a number such as 0, 1, 2, 3, and so on

word form: a number written in words; the word form for $3\frac{1}{6}$ is three and one-sixth.

Answer Keys

Meaning of Fractions (p. 4)

1. $\frac{3}{4}$ 2. $2\frac{3}{4}$ 3. $\frac{4}{4}$
4. four and two-thirds   5. five-sixths
6. six-fourths   7. one and three-tenths
8. two-halves   9. $10\frac{1}{6}$
10. $\frac{1}{4}$ 11. $12\frac{2}{3}$ 12. $\frac{9}{9}$ 13. $\frac{3}{4}$
14. $\frac{5}{3}$ 15. $\frac{6}{5}$

Simplifying Fractions (p. 6)

1. 1, 2, 3, 4, 6, 8, 12, and 24
2. 1, 2, 4, and 8
3. 1, 2, 3, 6, 9, and 18
4. 1, 2, 3, 4, 6, 8, 12, 16, 24, and 48
5. 1, 3, 5, 15, 25, and 75
6. 14   7. 6   8. 8   9. $\frac{3}{4}$
10. $\frac{3}{5}$ 11. $\frac{3}{7}$ 12. $\frac{2}{3}$ 13. $\frac{2}{3}$
14. $\frac{1}{2}$ 15. $\frac{2}{5}$ 16. $\frac{7}{18}$

Converting Mixed Numbers and Improper Fractions (p. 8)

1. $\frac{39}{5}$ 2. $\frac{17}{9}$ 3. $\frac{54}{5}$ 4. $\frac{17}{10}$
5. $\frac{20}{3}$ 6. $\frac{215}{70}$ 7. $\frac{59}{6}$ 8. $\frac{35}{8}$
9. $3\frac{1}{3}$ 10. 2   11. 1   12. $6\frac{1}{7}$
13. $7\frac{1}{4}$ 14. $7\frac{2}{3}$ 15. 1   16. $1\frac{9}{10}$
17. $\frac{19}{4}$
18. Multiply the whole number times the denominator and add the numerator. This is the new numerator over the same denominator.

Unit Assessment: Fraction Basics (p. 9–11)

1. c   2. b   3. b   4. d
5. c   6. b   7. c   8. c
9. a   10. d   11. d   12. b

Multiplying a Fraction by a Fraction (p. 12)

1. $\frac{35}{48}$ 2. $\frac{2}{5}$ 3. $\frac{9}{32}$ 4. $\frac{9}{50}$
5. $\frac{21}{40}$ 6. $\frac{7}{10}$ 7. $\frac{15}{32}$ 8. $\frac{8}{25}$

9. $\frac{5}{72}$ 10. $\frac{2}{5}$ 11. $\frac{7}{25}$ 12. $\frac{2}{3}$
13. $\frac{1}{4}$ 14. $\frac{21}{50}$ 15. $\frac{3}{16}$ 16. $\frac{8}{15}$
17. $\frac{4}{9}$ cup   18. Multiply $\frac{2}{3}$ by $\frac{2}{3}$.

Multiplying Fractions and Whole Numbers (p. 14)

1. 1   2. $11\frac{1}{2}$ 3. $\frac{1}{2}$
4. $10\frac{2}{3}$ 5. $5\frac{2}{3}$ 6. $4\frac{1}{2}$
7. $10\frac{1}{2}$ 8. $\frac{1}{2}$ 9. $11\frac{2}{5}$
10. $9\frac{1}{6}$ 11. $7\frac{3}{4}$ 12. $1\frac{1}{2}$
13. 5   14. $12\frac{1}{4}$ 15. $6\frac{3}{10}$
16. 28   17. $3\frac{1}{3}$ bushels
18. Multiply $\frac{10}{1}$ by $\frac{1}{3}$. Change the improper fraction $\frac{10}{3}$ to $3\frac{1}{3}$ by dividing 10 by 3 and putting the remainder over the divisor.

Multiplying Mixed Numbers (p. 16)

1. $12\frac{1}{2}$ 2. 15   3. $3\frac{8}{9}$
4. $3\frac{3}{5}$ 5. 6   6. $7\frac{7}{8}$
7. $3\frac{11}{18}$ 8. 9   9. 20
10. $12\frac{3}{8}$ 11. $12\frac{1}{4}$ 12. $11\frac{1}{4}$
13. $12\frac{1}{2}$ 14. $16\frac{2}{3}$ 15. 4
16. $4\frac{1}{8}$ 17. $4\frac{1}{5}$ miles
18. First, change both mixed numbers to improper fractions. Then, multiply the numerators and denominators. Change the improper fraction to a mixed number by dividing. Simplify the answer.

Multiplying Fractions and Mixed Numbers: A Shortcut (p. 18)

1. $\frac{3}{10}$ 2. $\frac{2}{9}$ 3. 3   4. $\frac{7}{15}$
5. $\frac{4}{5}$ 6. $\frac{3}{4}$ 7. $\frac{14}{15}$ 8. $\frac{9}{28}$

9. $1\frac{1}{10}$ **10.** $1\frac{1}{2}$ **11.** $\frac{3}{16}$ **12.** $2\frac{1}{2}$

13. $\frac{5}{18}$ **14.** $\frac{7}{15}$ **15.** 1 **16.** $2\frac{14}{27}$

17. 2 trays

18. Multiply $\frac{2}{3}$ by $\frac{3}{1}$. Cross-cancel. Answer is $\frac{2}{1}$ or simply 2.

Unit Assessment: Multiplying Fractions and Mixed Numbers (p. 19–20)

1. b **2.** a **3.** c **4.** b
5. c **6.** d **7.** b **8.** a
9. d **10.** b **11.** c **12.** c

Reciprocals (p. 22)

1. $\frac{7}{3}$ **2.** $\frac{8}{7}$ **3.** $\frac{1}{7}$ **4.** $\frac{6}{5}$

5. $\frac{5}{4}$ **6.** $\frac{3}{2}$ **7.** $\frac{1}{5}$ **8.** $\frac{12}{1}$

9. $\frac{4}{5}$ **10.** $\frac{4}{39}$ **11.** $\frac{1}{21}$ **12.** $\frac{2}{29}$

13. $\frac{5}{48}$ **14.** $\frac{1}{73}$ **15.** $\frac{6}{31}$ **16.** $\frac{3}{31}$

17. Convert the mixed number to an improper fraction and then invert it.

Dividing by Fractions (p. 24)

1. $2\frac{2}{3}$ **2.** $1\frac{2}{7}$ **3.** $1\frac{4}{5}$ **4.** $1\frac{7}{8}$

5. $\frac{8}{9}$ **6.** $\frac{15}{32}$ **7.** 1 **8.** $\frac{3}{8}$

9. $\frac{5}{8}$ **10.** $\frac{24}{35}$ **11.** $\frac{18}{25}$ **12.** 4

13. $\frac{5}{12}$ **14.** $\frac{1}{3}$ **15.** $\frac{1}{4}$ **16.** $\frac{3}{20}$

17. 3 scoops

18. Divide $\frac{1}{2}$ by $\frac{1}{6}$. Find the reciprocal of $\frac{1}{6}$ and multiply. $\frac{1}{2} \times \frac{6}{1} = \frac{6}{2}$. Divide the improper fraction. The answer is 3.

Dividing Whole Numbers and Mixed Numbers (p. 26)

1. 5 **2.** $\frac{5}{16}$ **3.** $\frac{3}{8}$ **4.** 2

5. 3 **6.** $1\frac{2}{7}$ **7.** 8 **8.** $\frac{25}{36}$

9. 10 **10.** $\frac{9}{10}$ **11.** $3\frac{1}{8}$ **12.** $4\frac{1}{2}$

13. $\frac{9}{35}$ **14.** $\frac{5}{6}$ **15.** 6 **16.** 24

17. 8 hours

18. Divide 12 inches by $1\frac{1}{2}$ inches per hour. If possible, simplify the answer.

Unit Assessment: Dividing Fractions and Mixed Numbers (p. 27–28)

1. b **2.** a **3.** d **4.** c
5. b **6.** a **7.** d **8.** c
9. a **10.** a **11.** b **12.** c

Converting Decimals to Fractions (p. 30)

1. $\frac{23}{100}$ **2.** $\frac{6}{100}$ **3.** $\frac{7}{10}$

4. $\frac{13}{1000}$ **5.** $\frac{74}{1000}$ **6.** $\frac{88}{100}$

7. $\frac{9}{10}$ **8.** $\frac{34}{1000}$ **9.** $3\frac{7}{10}$

10. $18\frac{8}{100}$ **11.** $47\frac{73}{1000}$ **12.** $17\frac{5}{10}$

13. $4\frac{1}{1000}$ **14.** $5\frac{62}{100}$ **15.** $50\frac{1}{10}$

16. $36\frac{19}{100}$ **17.** $\frac{9}{10}$ **18.** $179\frac{35}{100}$

Converting Fractions to Decimals (p. 32)

1. 0.1 **2.** 0.37 **3.** 0.08
4. 0.3 **5.** 7.01 **6.** 0.007
7. 13.1 **8.** 0.064 **9.** 0.17
10. 47.9 **11.** 57.84 **12.** 506.073
13. 112.69 **14.** 27.3 **15.** 9.009
16. 2.35
17. eighty-seven and four-thousandths
18. 93.67

Divide to Convert Fractions to Decimals (p.34)

1. 0.4 **2.** 0.125 **3.** 0.08
4. 0.75 **5.** 0.5 **6.** 0.6
7. 0.25 **8.** 0.45 **9.** 0.5625
10. 0.2 **11.** 0.625 **12.** 0.875
13. 0.375 **14.** 0.8 **15.** 0.06
16. 0.4375 **17.** 0.25 **18.** 0.6

Unit Assessment: Fractions and Decimals (p. 35–36)

1. d **2.** a **3.** d **4.** b
5. b **6.** c **7.** a **8.** d
9. c **10.** c **11.** b **12.** a

Converting Fractions to Percents (p. 38)
1. 15%   2. 29%   3. 8%
4. 1%   5. 62%   6. 99%
7. 13%   8. 56%   9. 40%
10. 25%   11. 50%   12. 75%
13. 60%   14. 16%   15. 45%
16. 34%   17. 12%   18. 45%

Probability (p. 40)
1. $\frac{1}{8}$ 2. $\frac{1}{4}$ 3. $\frac{3}{4}$ 4. $\frac{1}{2}$
5. $\frac{2}{19}$ 6. $\frac{2}{19}$ 7. $\frac{4}{19}$ 8. $\frac{2}{3}$
9. $\frac{2}{3}$ 10. 40 times

Meaning of Ratios (p. 42)
1. $\frac{1}{2}$ 2. 1:2   3. 0.5   4. 50%

5. $\frac{\text{students absent}}{\text{total students}} = \frac{3}{30}$ 6. $\frac{\text{wing flaps}}{\text{seconds}} = \frac{60}{1}$

7. $\frac{\text{quarters}}{\text{dollars}} = \frac{4}{1}$ 8. $\frac{\text{hours worked}}{\text{total hours}} = \frac{8}{24}$

9. $\frac{\text{pizzas}}{\text{cost}} = \frac{3}{\$15.00}$ 10. $\frac{\text{miles traveled}}{\text{hours}} = \frac{213}{4}$

11. $\frac{\text{ears of corn}}{\text{cost}} = \frac{10}{\$1.00}$ 12. $\frac{\text{strokes}}{\text{meters}} = \frac{8}{5}$

13. $\frac{\text{push-ups}}{\text{seconds}} = \frac{2}{3}$ 14. $\frac{\text{cups}}{\text{cans}} = \frac{2}{1}$

15. $\frac{\text{cups}}{\text{gallons}} = \frac{16}{1}$ 16. $\frac{\text{cans}}{\text{price}} = \frac{6}{79¢}$

Finding Equivalent Ratios (p. 44)
1. $\frac{4}{2} = \frac{6}{3} = \frac{8}{4} = \frac{10}{5} = \frac{12}{6}$
2. $\frac{10}{6} = \frac{15}{9} = \frac{20}{12} = \frac{25}{15} = \frac{30}{18}$
3. $\frac{4}{\$50.00} = \frac{6}{\$75.00} = \frac{8}{\$100.00} = \frac{10}{\$125.00} = \frac{12}{\$150.00}$
4. $\frac{6}{30} = \frac{9}{45} = \frac{12}{60} = \frac{15}{75} = \frac{18}{90}$
5. $\frac{90}{18} = \frac{135}{27} = \frac{180}{36} = \frac{225}{45} = \frac{270}{54}$

6. 7 teams   7. 125 baseballs
8. 8 pies   9. 49 sit-ups
10. 9 hits

Finding Missing Numbers and Cross-Products of Ratios (p. 46)
1. $n = 5$ 2. $n = 32$ 3. $n = 10$
4. $n = 16$ 5. $n = 9$ 6. $n = 8$
7. $n = 10$ 8. no   9. no
10. yes   11. no   12. yes
13. no   14. no   15. 3,120 km
16. 130 km   17. 15 glasses

Unit Assessment: Percents/Probability/Ratios (p. 47–48)
1. c   2. d   3. b   4. c
5. c   6. d   7. a   8. a
9. b   10. d   11. b   12. b

Learning Station One: Probability (p. 50)
1. $\frac{3}{8}$ 2. a. 3 draws
                     b. 12 draws
                     c. 30 draws
                     d. 36 draws

Learning Station Two: Take a Poll (p. 51)
Answers will vary.

Learning Station Three: Sugar Cookie Recipe (p. 52)
1. $4\frac{1}{2}$ cups   2. 6 cups
3. 12 eggs   4. $2\frac{1}{4}$ teaspoons
5. $3\frac{3}{4}$ cups   6. $\frac{3}{4}$ teaspoon
7. Add or multiply   8. $\frac{\text{sugar}}{\text{eggs}} = \frac{2}{4}$ or $\frac{1}{2}$
9. $\frac{\text{baking powder}}{\text{salt}} = \frac{3/4}{1/4}$
10. $1\frac{1}{4}$ teaspoons
11. My friend divided incorrectly. He should have put the remainder over the divisor to come up with $1\frac{1}{4}$ teaspoon, not 1 teaspoon.

Learning Station Four: Using Pictures to Multiply Fractions (p. 53)

1. $\frac{1}{12}$ 2. $\frac{1}{9}$ 3. $\frac{4}{15}$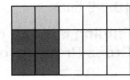

4. $\frac{3}{10}$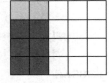

5. $\frac{1}{4}$ 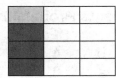 6. $\frac{5}{12}$

Daily Math Review #1 (p. 54)
1. 52 ounces 2. 0.125 3. 4
4. $\frac{3}{10}$ 5. 14

Daily Math Review #2 (p. 54)
1. 10 feet 2. 0.64 3. 125 baskets
4. $\frac{9}{64}$ 5. $7\frac{1}{3}$

Daily Math Review #3 (p. 54)
1. 1,600 pounds 2. 0.75 3. $\frac{5}{37}$
4. $7\frac{7}{9}$ 5. $8\frac{1}{3}$

Daily Math Review #4 (p. 54)
1. $8.44 2. 0.333 3. 27
4. $2\frac{14}{27}$ 5. $3\frac{1}{3}$

Daily Math Review #5 (p. 55)
1. $31.32 2. $\frac{21}{100}$ 3. $\frac{12}{9}$
4. $\frac{5}{14}$ 5. 10

Daily Math Review #6 (p. 55)
1. 9.6 inches 2. $4\frac{36}{100}$ 3. $n = 36$
4. $\frac{7}{27}$ 5. $\frac{5}{6}$

Daily Math Review #7 (p. 55)
1. $306\frac{2}{3}$ gallons 2. 0.7 3. 25%
4. $10\frac{2}{3}$ 5. $6\frac{6}{35}$

Daily Math Review #8 (p. 55)
1. 350 acres 2. $22\frac{5}{100}$ 3. 60%
4. 1 5. $5\frac{5}{11}$

Daily Math Review #9 (p. 56)
1. $4\frac{8}{9}$ ounces 2. $n = 4$ 3. $\frac{4}{15}$
4. $\frac{21}{80}$ 5. $1\frac{5}{8}$

Daily Math Review #10 (p. 56)
1. 4 students 2. 6 3. 20%
4. 75 5. 7

Daily Math Review #11 (p. 56)
1. $\frac{3}{5}$ 2. 24 stones 3. $5\frac{25}{100}$
4. $4\frac{1}{8}$ 5. $2\frac{11}{14}$

Daily Math Review #12 (p. 56)
1. $\frac{13}{21}$ or 13:21 2. $n = 12$ 3. $\frac{9}{6}$
4. $4\frac{1}{56}$ 5. $3\frac{43}{51}$

Daily Math Review #13 (p. 57)
1. $6\frac{1}{2}$ ounces 2. $n = 24$
3. $\frac{strokes}{meters} = \frac{9}{6}$ 4. $\frac{1}{4}$ 5. $6\frac{2}{5}$

Daily Math Review #14 (p. 57)
1. 16 years old
2. $\frac{bales}{days} = \frac{4}{2} = \frac{6}{3} = \frac{8}{4}$
3. $\frac{8}{57}$ 4. $\frac{1}{4}$ 5. $36\frac{4}{7}$

Daily Math Review #15 (p. 57)
1. 8 servings 2. $\frac{6}{10} = \frac{9}{15} = \frac{12}{20}$
3. 0.03 4. 1 5. $3\frac{2}{3}$

Daily Math Review #16 (p. 57)
1. 2 donuts 2. two and three-fifths
3. no 4. 120 5. 16